Recollections *and* Reflections *of*

MOLLIE HANSFORD

1828–1900

Revised Edition by WILLIAM D. WINTZ

Pictorical Histories Publishing Company, Inc.
Charleston, West Virginia

Mollie Hansford Walls Rust with grandsons Kenneth Schultz and Hugo Walls. AC

*It had been impressed on my mind for some time
that I should writedown the many incidents of my life
for my children and grandchildren. In years
to come it may be a pleasure and possibly
a benefit to them in some way.*

LIBRARY OF CONGRESS
CATALOG CARD NO. 96-69799

ISBN 1-57510-017-7

PRINTED IN U.S.A.

First Printing August 1975
Second Printing October 1996

Typography & Book Design
Arrow Graphics

Cover Art
William D. Wintz

PICTORIAL HISTORIES PUBLISHING CO.
4103 Virginia Ave., SE
Charleston, West Virginia 25304

Contents

Preface

ARY JANE "MOLLIE" Hansford was born at the mouth of Paint Creek on the Kanawha River in 1828. She was the daughter of John and Elizabeth Teays Hansford. Her father's parents were Major John and Jane Morris Hansford and her mother was the daughter of Stephen and Mary Carroll Teays. Mollie was truly a daughter of the Kanawha Frontier since the Hansfords, Teays, Morrises and Carrolls were all original settlers in the valley. They all came during the Indian Wars and each family had more than one encounter with the Red men.

Mollie's mother died when she was only ten months old and she was taken to Coalsmouth, now St. Albans, to be cared for by her mother's family. When she was three, however, her father remarried and she was brought back home to Paint Creek.

When she was seven, the Hansfords moved to Coalsmouth and Mollie lived there from 1835 to 1853. It was then that she married Dr. John W. Walls and went to live at Newtown, near Winchester, in the Shenandoah valley of Virginia.

This book of Mollie's recollections and reflections only covers her life before she was married. She later wrote a separate account of her life during the Civil War which she titled "Reminiscence of the War." These writings, along with those of her sister, Victoria, have been edited and published by this author under the title "The Civil War Memoirs of Two Rebel Sisters."

By describing in detail events first hand and the life styles and customs of the people of her time, Mollie Hansford Walls has given us a clearer and more profound understanding of our traditional and historical heritage.

The editorial comments of the author have been added only to give present-day emphasis to the historical value of her writings.

Prologue

The First Seven Pages

A NUMBER OF YEARS ago an elderly member of our church congregation whose name was Hugo Walls passed away. He had lived by himself in a small trailer and the few members of his family in the area asked the church for help in disposing of his effects. I was one of the volunteers, and with family members we began to sort out the contents of his trailer. We soon discovered he had been a great reader and every available space was taken up with books. Even an old hump-back trunk on the ground under the trailer was found filled with reading material.

On the very bottom of the trunk was a badly damaged hand-written manuscript lying face down. Since the trunk was on the bare ground, the first seven pages had drawn moisture and were completely illegible. On examination by family members, it was determined that the manuscript had been written by Hugo Walls' grandmother, Mollie Hansford Walls.

With the help and permission of her great-granddaughter, Mary Sue Woodson, I was able to transcribe the manuscript and edit it for a limited publication. Soon after the book had been distributed I received a call from Russell L. Hansford of Marmet, West Virginia. He informed me that he had the first seven pages of Mollie Hansford's manuscript. How could that be? We had the original manuscript and the first seven pages were completely destroyed.

Mr. Hansford explained that he had a great aunt, Kathrine Hansford who had visited Mollie's family soon after her death and had the opportunity to copy her recollections. Since Mr. Hansford had inherited his aunt's papers he had found the copy among them. Therefore, this revised edition now contains the first seven pages of Mollie's Recollections and Reflections.

Katherine S. Hansford, 1875–1963, noted the following comment on her copy: "Cousin Mollie was such a dear aristocratic old lady, she always wore lovely black lace caps. I visited at her home in the summer of 1893, how I wish at that time I had realized the importance of seeking family history."

Acknowledgments

THIS BOOK IS A TRIBUTE to the remarkable pioneer Hansford family who helped set the course of history of the Great Kanawha Valley. Their frontier, deeds, the character of their people, and the writings of their descendants have opened a door to the past that we knew very little about.

Special appreciation is extended to other Hansford family descendants who have contributed directly to this book. They include Mary Sue Woodson, Russell L. Hansford, Hester M. Graham, and Nancy B. Bell.

To friends and associates who have provided helpful assistance and encouragement, I am also indebted. They include Richard Andre, Noble Wyatt, Dennis Deitz, Stan Cohen, Elizabeth Green and Bill Williams.

A special thanks is extended to Frederick Armstrong and his staff of the West Virginia Department of Archives and History. They were always willing to help with special assistance, and their sound judgement and opinions were appreciated.

Especially, I am grateful to my wife Ruth who typed and retyped the manuscript and was still able to maintain her usual cheerful disposition.

Dedication

*This book is sincerely dedicated
to all my many friends
and associates
I have come to know through
a common interest
in West Virginia History.*

1

Family Background

JOHN HANSFORD, my father, was born and raised at the mouth of Paint Creek, Kanawha County, West Virginia. He was the sixth son of John Hansford, Sr. who married Jane Morris, the eldest daughter of Major William and Catherine Carroll Morris. Jane Morris's sisters were Mrs. Catherine Venable and Mrs. Cynthia Noyes. Soon after their marriage her father gave her about fifteen hundred acres of land including the mouth of Paint Creek and extending along the Kanawha River where several large coal mines are now located.

They built a cabin where Crown Hill mines are now operating. My grandmother has often told me of her early married life. She said she had to look out for Indians while her Johnny cleared and ploughed, but that she never saw but one hostile Indian. The white people were getting too thick for them, and after the first year of their married life they had no more trouble with them.

Her father had given her two slaves, a man and a woman both very young and they were of great help and comfort. They soon had a nice little farm cleared. They raised all they had to eat except meat. They depended mostly on the wild game that filled the surrounding woods. They had bear meat and venison cured for winter as we do pork now. There was always plenty of fresh meat of all kinds, wild turkey, pheasants, and partridges which were as common as our tame ones are now.

As the years rolled on she said the children came fast, both black and white. There was a great deal of work to be done but soon there were more hands to do it. Children in those days were taught to work young, there was always something they could do, from the time they were five years old.

My grandmother said all their clothing was made at home. She said we raised cotton, hemp and flax, but mostly flax from which we made linen for household purposes. We raised sheep for the wool and it kept our women busy summer and winter, carding and spinning and weaving.

I have seen my grandmother herself spinning. She told me that she spun and wove her own wedding dress. She said it was so fine she could pull the warp thru her wedding ring. When it was woven it was the color of unbleached brown linen. She said she bleached it herself, then cut and made the dress.

My grandfather, John Hansford, had eleven sons and one daughter, all born and raised on the farm or plantation at Paint Creek. They all worked on the farm or got out timber to build flat boats that were sold to the salt makers at what was then called "The Licks" (now Malden).

Grandfather planted large apple and peach orchards and made quantities of apple and peach brandy, yet not one of his eleven sons ever drank to excess; no one ever saw one intoxicated. His oldest son Hiram enlisted in the Army in 1812 and went to Norfolk, Virginia, but was never in a battle.

As the sons came of age grandfather gave them their choice to stay home and work for wages or he would give them money enough to go wherever they wished. If they stayed home, however, and did not work, they had to pay their board as regular strangers. Three of his sons went West; Hiram went to Missouri, William went to Kentucky, and Charles went to Knoxville, Illinois. All married after they left home and had families.

All the rest of his sons remained on the Kanawha. There were three old bachelors,

Carroll, Alvah, and Marshall. All three built nice homes and lived in them alone. Felix Gilbert, the only one who had a middle name, married Miss Sallie Frazier of Lewisburg in Greenbrier County.

My grandfather Hansford was a member of the Virginia Legislature for many years. He would go to Richmond on horseback and it would take a week. His house was on the only road that crossed this part of the state and he always at that time kept entertainment. All men going to Legislature or Congress, or looking for land would stop with him as he was well fixed to entertain them. A large house with stables was scarce in those days. He was also Magistrate for thirty years.

His youngest son Milton married Mary Parks, a great niece of George Washington. Her parents were dead and she was living with her aunt, Mrs. Shrewsbsury, at the time of her marriage. Gallatin Hansford married Miss Nancy Harriman, who lived several miles below the large farm and her father was John Harriman.

Morris Hansford was older than either of the sons I have just mentioned. He married his cousin, Miss Kitty Morris, daughter of William Morris, the brother of my grandmother, Jane Morris Hansford. Their mother was Catherine Carroll Morris.

John Hansford, my father, married Miss Elizabeth Teays, daughter of Stephen Teays who lived at the mouth of Coal River, now St. Albans. Her mother was Miss Mary Carroll, cousin to Mrs. Catherine Carroll Morris (wife of William). Therefore, Elizabeth Teays was a second cousin to John Hansford.

They were married on her seventeenth birthday which was December 25, 1827. I was born the following November 23, 1828. They went immediately to housekeeping on Paint Creek about one mile from the mouth where my father had a small grist mill. My grandmother Teays gave mother a Negro woman named Sucky to do the work and a little girl Jane about five as company for me.

My mother was so young and childish, and it was a wild and lonely place where they lived. Their house was on the creek bank and she would spend a great deal of time at the creek gathering wild flowers, shells and pebbles as a child would do. She would get her feet wet and sit for hours on the large rocks. In that way she caught a severe cold when I was just a few months old. They thought nothing of it as she was always so well. Even after it settled in her lungs, they never regarded it as serious.

My grandmother later told me she came down to her house walking with the Negro woman carrying me and it was nearly three miles. When she came in she complained of being so tired and feeling badly, although she looked so well and her cheeks were rosy. It was beautiful weather and they were sitting on the porch. Grandmother said "Betsy go in and lie down on my bed and rest, you must stay all night." She did so but never left it again as she had not been there but a few minutes when she had a severe hemorrhage. They looked for her to die all night but she lived several weeks. They sent for her two single sisters, Parthenia and Martha Teays, who lived at the mouth of Coal with my grandmother Teays. They came and stayed with her until her death.

She was only nineteen and my grandmother told me often that she thought her one of the most devoted Christians she ever knew. She would say "I am a Baptist and she was a Methodist, but I can say we never thought of the differences in churches then." I hope to be a true Christian when I come to die.

Her sisters asked "Bettie, who do you want to take your baby, Mary Jane to raise?" Her answer was "Leave her in the hands of the Lord, he knows best." After her death she was taken down to Coalsmouth and buried in the Teays family graveyard. It was a great undertaking at that time being over thirty miles. The coffin was put in a large canoe with two Negro men to push and my father and some others in the family to pilot and direct. My Uncle Alvah Hansford took my Aunt Martha and myself in what was at that time called a gigg. It was a two-wheeled vehicle which I suppose now is what we would call a cart. He has told me how near they came to turning over several times and killing me as the roads were so awful. The canoe arrived there long before we did.

My father returned to his home on Paint Creek leaving me with my grandmother and two aunts who had all the care of me. I was just eight months old and a delicate child. I was a great care and trouble and my aunts have since told me that no one thought I could possibly live for a year or more. I had to be carried on a pillow I was so small and emaciated. I was fed by fixing a goose quill through a cork and then wrapped with a soft cloth. A lady traveling stopped at my grandmother's and seeing me told them to stop giving me milk for a while and start giving me mutton broth with no grease on it. Only once in a while give me fresh milk just from the cow. From that time on I began to improve.

When I was three years old my father married the second time. He married his Cousin Maria Morris, a daughter of Carroll Morris who was drowned in the Kanawha River just above the mouth of Paint Creek. Maria and my mother had been great friends and after their marriage I was taken home.

By then my father had given up the mill and moved across the Kanawha on the Charleston side, between there and Kanawha Falls and almost opposite the mouth of Paint Creek. Here he opened a store and kept what was then called a stage stand. It was on the James River and Kanawha Turnpike and there was a line of stages running through to Richmond. These regular stands along the road were where they stopped for meals and to change horses. This was considered an elegant way of traveling in those days.

My step-mother was a very practical business woman. I know now when I look back and remember what a manager she was. The Negro woman Sucky, who had belonged to my mother, died soon after her mistress did. My grandmother Teays then gave Jane to me and she came with me to my father's as my maid. In the meantime my father bought a Negro woman with two children from my Uncle Felix and also his father had given him a man. Therefore, they had plenty of help and they always had a nice breakfast ready for the passengers on the stage.

The driver would blow his horn very loud and long before they came in sight if there were men passengers. I remember seeing Henry Clay and Thomas Benton as my father pointed them out to me.

My father was one of the most patient men with children. It was natural for me to cling to him at first after leaving my aunts where I had been petted and spoiled. I well remember the first whipping my step-mother ever gave me. It was for disobeying her and for running after and crying for father. She made the Negro girl bring me back and after giving me a keen little switching she set me on a stool in the corner. She then took two knitting needles and put on stitches to teach me to knit. I soon learned to stitch and knit myself a pair of garters. From that time I was always knitting in bad weather when I could not go to school.

Statues of Henry Clay & Thomas Benton

When Mollie Hansford saw Henry Clay and Thomas Benton together it must have been about 1834. Benton was a Congressman from Missouri while Clay represented Kentucky. Not only were they political cohorts, Thomas Benton was a cousin of Henry Clay's wife. It is a remarkable historical coincidence that statues of both men are standing side by side in the Statuary Hall of the United States Capitol; especially, since each state is only allowed to honor two of their favorite sons in the Great Hall. AC

Pioneer Schooling

I WENT TO SCHOOL when I was six years old to a Mr. Charles Anderson. His father and brothers had rented a salt furnace and coal mine from Grandfather Hansford. They were the first men who ever shipped coal from Kanawha in flat boats. I had neglected to say my grandfather had found salt water on his place and sunk two wells 650 feet deep. This was in 1823-24 and they had not found coal yet but ran the furnaces with wood.

I also forgot to say that in 1825 my father went to Lewisburg to an academy conducted by Rev. McElhany, a Presbyterian minister. There he obtained all the education he had which was considered good at that time.

I had to cross the river to go to school. Father would take me across every morning in a canoe and I would carry my dinner in a little bucket. I did not learn very much as I was a very timid child. If the teacher spoke cross I was afraid to say a word.

My step-mother had a little girl named Letitia, her first child. When she was about one year old and I was about four, we both took scarlet fever and she died. While they were gone to bury her they left me with Tildia, the Negro woman, and two neighbor women. I can remember they came to my bed and looking down at me one said "Poor little thing, she will be dead before they get back." They all then sat down to talk and have a smoke. I never opened my eyes or spoke, but as young as I was, I never forgot it.

Soon after I got well Father took me on a visit to see my Grandmother Teays. We went down to Coalsmouth on the stage and it was the first time I ever rode on one. The swinging motion made me very sick and I threw up on my pretty white dress, I called it my dumpling dress.

I can remember as if it was today that on our way we had to cross a ferry boat at Charleston, worked by horses on the opposite side. When the stage went to drive on to the boat it lurched out from the shore causing all the stage horses to fall back into the water. The driver finally got them cut loose but not before they were all drowned. The stage was left standing full of water and my father threw me to a man on the bank. All the other passengers were also saved. We were all taken to the Goshorn Tavern that was near the ferry. I think it was owned and run by Old Man George Goshorn, as they called him at that time. He had some five or six sons that I always remembered as ferrymen in after years.

I did not go to Coalsmouth often as both of my mother's sisters were soon married. Parthenia married Mr. Sam Wilson who was a son of "Irish Jimmie Wilson" as he was called. Martha married Joseph Capehart when they both were quite young. My Grandmother Teays still lived at the old home at the mouth of Coal River, on the bank of the Kanawha. Her husband Stephen Teays had owned all the land on the lower side of Coal River to as far down as Scary Creek and up Coal as far as the falls. He had left it all to Grandmother to divide with the children when they were of age.

Grandfather Teays had three sons but William died before he did. The other two, James and John, lived to be old men but John never married. James married Eliza Everett, daughter of Col. John Everett of Guyandotte. They lived at what was called Coal Bridge, about a mile above the mouth of the river on the James River and Kanawha Pike. He built a large tavern house just at the bridge but always rented it out. He also built himself a cottage just across the road with a store house beside it where he kept store for many years.

Just around from the bridge were several houses, a blacksmith shop and a tailor shop, it was quite a little village. It was a large covered wooden bridge and everyone who crossed paid toll. My Uncle James Teays collected on his side of the river and Col. Phil Thompson collected on the other side.

My Aunt Mary, or "Polly" as she was called, married John Capehart and his older brother Joe married Aunt Martha. The two brothers had come up the river on a store boat and landed it at the mouth of Coal where they stayed until they had married the Teays sisters. Grandmother gave them both a farm and a Negro or two a piece. John was a business man and he built himself a little storehouse and left his boat and he went to selling goods as well as farming. He soon built himself a fine brick home which is still standing and he gradually became what in those days was considered a rich man.

John and Polly Capehart had three sons and one daughter. When Aunt Polly died they had taken their niece to live with them. She was a daughter of my Aunt Katherine Teays who had married a Thomas and they both had died. They had left three children, two daughters and a son. Mary Ann lived with Aunt Polly, Elizabeth lived with Uncle James Teays and the son, Stephen, went West to live with his Uncle Nob Thomas where he died in Indiana. Elizabeth never married and Mary Ann married her second cousin, James Teays, a son of John Teays of Lynchburg. He came out here on a visit to his relations. After her marriage, Mary Ann continued to keep house for Uncle John Capehart until he had married the second time. By then Aunt Polly had died and Uncle John had needed someone to care for his children. He said now it was natural that Mary Ann should want to go to housekeeping for herself. Her mother had left a nice little farm at Guyandotte and they moved on that. She had one Negro woman and her husband had a man.

Elizabeth Thomas still continued to live with her Uncle James Teays until he moved to Missouri, then she went to live with her sister Mary Ann. She took care of the children and was as devoted to them as their mother. She had several offers of marriage but seemed never to care for gentlemen's society. She was beloved by everyone and everyone was always glad to see Miss Lizzie Thomas coming. I have heard several persons say she was a model and if all old maids were as cheerful and happy as she was they never would advise marriage.

Uncle John Capehart's second wife was a Miss Betsy Rogers. She came from Fauguier County, Virginia with the Chiltons, several brothers moved to Kanawha at the same time. She kept house for Mark Chilton who was a widower and had rented Grandmother's old house at the Mouth of Coal. Here is where John Capehart married her. She was an excellent housekeeper and a strong minded business woman who raised the children well. Uncle John was in bad health for years before his death and she was kind and good to him.

She was a very ambitious woman and fond of display. As he was well off and they lived in a fine house, she had a good opportunity of entertaining in style and making a great show in keeping up with the leaders of society. She had taken her brother and sister to live with her. Although they had been very poor they were of a good family and were well educated. Her sister, Miss Mary Rogers, was as refined and nice lady as I ever knew. She never married and lived to a very old age.

Uncle John Capehart went to the White Sulphur Springs nearly every summer. He died at White Sulphur August 5, 1846, and was brought home on the stage to be buried in the Teays Burying Ground. His oldest son, William, was at the time with his Uncle James Capehart at Point Pleasant and there were none of them of age at the time.

A*T LEAST THREE Chilton brothers came to the Kanawha Valley about 1826. They were Blackwell, Samuel, and Mark. Blackwell and Sarah (Gibson) Chilton had four children who married into the Wilson family of Coalsmouth. Samuel B. Wilson was their father and their mother was Parthenia (Teays) Wilson, a sister of Mollie Hansford's mother. Therefore, she was related to most of the Wilsons and Chiltons.*

Mary Teays married John Capehart and Martha Teays married Joseph Capehart. Since they were also sisters of Mollie's mother, many of the Capeharts were also her relatives. — Laidley; History of Charleston and Kanawha Co., W. Va. Hist. Mag., July 1903, p. 293.

Aunt Betsy continued to keep house at the old home sending the children to school. Thenie, the only daughter, was boarded at Mr. Frank Thompson's, to be instructed with his daughters, who always had a fine governess. the one they had at that time was Miss Annie Barnett, a fine music teacher. (As well as I remember she was from Newark, New Jersey.) Thenie had a piano which was considered a great thing in those days. She became a good performer and afterwards went to school in Point Pleasant.

About this time her step-mother married again, the Rev. Sam Wyatt of the Baptist Church and moved to Buffalo, Putnam County, to live. She is still living, over 94 years old. Her second husband having been dead over thirty years and the only living son of her first husband is taking care of her.

When Mollie Hansford was 10 months old, her mother Elizabeth (Teays) Hansford died at the early age of nineteen. Her father was remarried soon after to his first cousin, Maria Morris, daughter of Carroll Morris, his mother's brother. By this marriage they had four children, namely: Charles V., born 1834; Carroll M., born 1836; Victoria F., born 1838; and Cinthia N., born 1841. (Hansford family Bible; W. Va. Hist. Mag., July 1903.

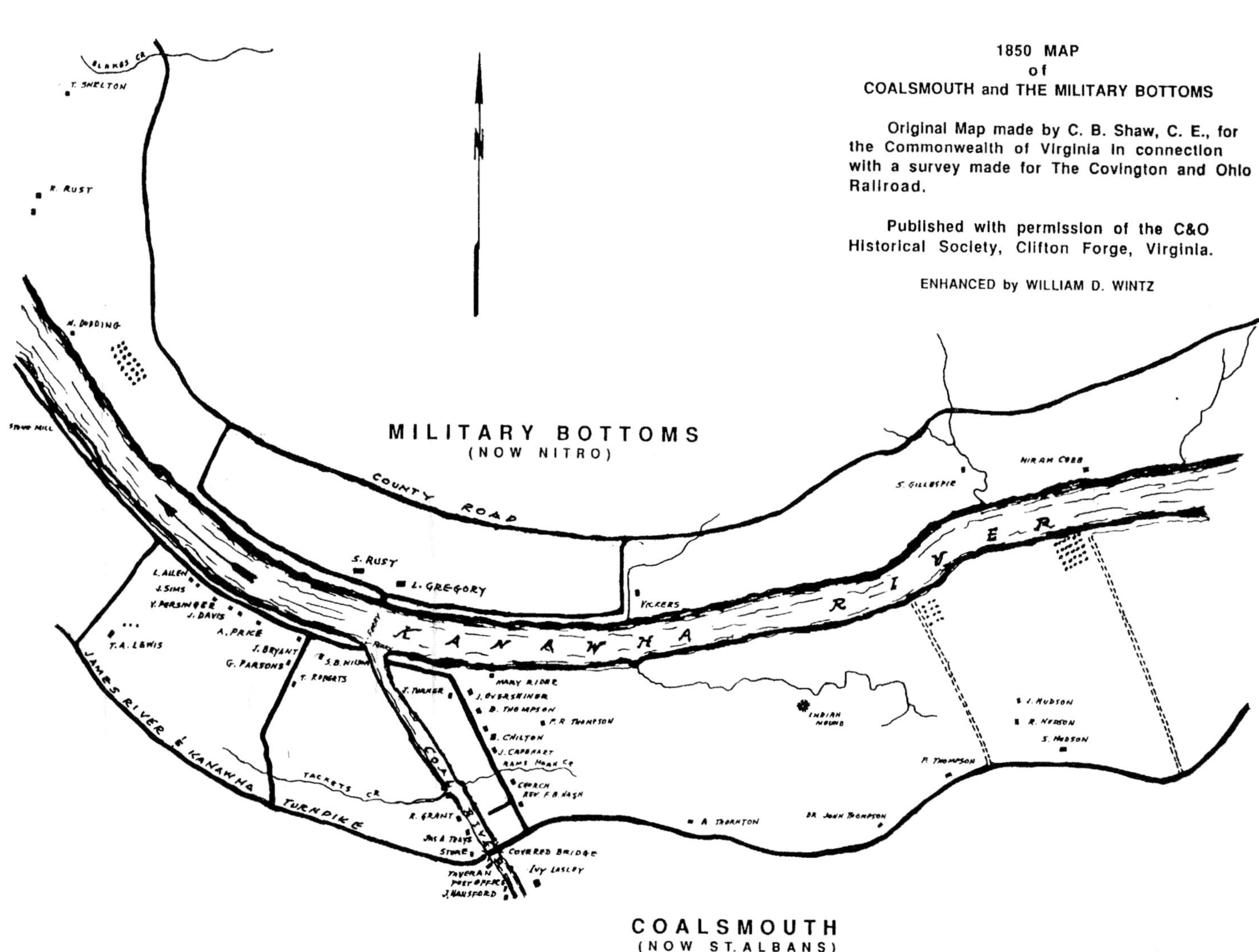

3

Growing Up In Coalsmouth

WHEN I WAS SEVEN years old I had two little half brothers, Charles V. and Carroll M., the last was a babe of one year. It was then that I was sent to school at the "Licks" (Malden) where my step-mother's sister lived. I boarded with a family named Shelton, a man and his wife. One room of the house was a large old store room, gloomy and dark with one window and my little bed was put in this room. Mrs. Shelton, or the black girl, would go with me, with a tallow candle, to see me in bed and then take the candle away. I would cover up my head and be frightened almost to death until I would go to sleep. Little do grown people think how children suffer from fear.

I spent a sad time here, the man and his wife were always quarrelling and she never let me go out. She was so hard and cruel to the black girl that one day I went in the kitchen and found her hanging to the rafters. Mrs. Shelton was so frightened she fainted. I ran for her husband who was at work at his shop.

The only pleasure I had there was in receiving things from home. Father went to Pittsburgh for goods and one morning the stage driver stopped and called that there was a box for me. It was a very small trunk covered with black leather and studded with brass tacks. I thought it was the most beautiful thing I ever saw. It had a key, and on opening it I found all kinds of confectionery, oranges and fig candies, everything to please a child. Two beautiful dolls, one my father gave me and one my Uncle James Teays sent me. He and my father had gone together to lay in a stock of goods. At that time all the merchants bought their goods at Pittsburgh, Cincinnati was a small town then.

Soon after this my father and step-mother came down on a visit to her sister's and found how I was situated. They then took me to Charleston to attend a girls' school conducted by the Rev. James Brown, a Presbyterian minister, who was assisted by a Miss Howe. I was in her department with all the small children.

Mollie Hansford was attending Mercer Academy in Charleston as Dr. James Brown was the director of the school at that time. It was established as a joint stock company by the citizens of Charleston in 1818 and continued until the beginning of the Civil War in 1861.

Dr. James M. Brown was pastor of the First Presbyterian Church of Charleston from 1837 until his death in 1862. In 1786 his mother was taken by the Indians during the Abbs Valley raid and was a witness to the brutal murders of most of her family. She was finally returned after being held captive by the Indians for over three years. She lived to marry Samuel Brown and to become the mother of five Presbyterian ministers, including Dr. James Moore Brown. —History of the Great Kanawha Valley, p. 253; History of the Presbytery of Kanawha, p. 102.

I boarded at Mrs. Norris Whittaker's, sister of my step-mother. She had two small children and it was unlike my last boarding place, I never got lonely. I had to get up every morning, dress myself and the two children before breakfast. As they lived at the extreme lower end of town, I had to take my dinner and stay at the school house at noon all alone, as none of the other girls brought their lunch.

I shall always remember one girl with love as she would often beg her mother to let her stay with me. She would bring a nice lunch to share and I enjoyed it very much. I had very little given me as Mrs. Whittaker would leave it to the Negro girl to put up my lunch. Many times

Rogers Pharmacy and neighbors on early Front Street.
FROM PIONEERS AND THEIR HOMES ON UPPER KANAWHA.

I had nothing but a pone of corn bread split in two with maybe a little butter on it. Or a slice of fat meat, always such fare as the Negroes had in the kitchen. (I always called Mrs. Whittaker Aunt Lueticia and her husband Uncle Norris.)

Mary Brooks, the girl that was so good to me, was the only daughter of Mr. Brooks, a salt maker who was considered very wealthy, she was about my age. I suffered many heart aches at this school as all the girls dressed fine and my clothes were very plain. The girls would often make fun of my blue calico dress and Mary would always stand up for me and sit beside me in school.

There was another person who was always kind to me. It was old Mrs. Whittaker who lived near the school. She would often send for me to come over and get my dinner if she had any extra little things. Her favorite dessert for her boys was pancakes with sugar and butter between them. No one but a little child as I was, can understand how I loved those two friends, and remembered them ever afterwards.

It was my work when I went home in the evening to scrub all the tableware for supper. One evening I went out on a pile of lumber that was in the yard to wash them. In looking down I saw underneath some boards a tin pan that held a quart or more, it was full of damson preserves. I ran in the house and told Mrs. Whittaker about it. She went out to see and told me not to disturb it. She said she would find out who stole it as she had been making a large kettle of those preserves out in the yard the day before. She told me to get my bonnet as she wanted me to go up the street for her. She gave me the money with a note to the drug store. I afterwards learned she sent for "Tarteremetic." When I returned she took the paper and sprinkled the contents in the pan of preserves and stirred it up and then returned it to the same place.

That night one of the Negro men that Uncle Norris had hired was taken very ill and seemed to get no better, after vomiting awfully. Uncle started for the doctor when Mrs. Whittaker told him what she had done, to find out who stole her preserves. He was very angry and told her if the man died he would have to pay for him.

Dr. Henry Rogers came to Charleston about 1814 and established Charleston's first drug store. After the death of Dr. Rogers in 1837, his son J. H. Rogers, an able businessman, salt maker, inventor, and collector of historical documents and records, followed as owner of the pharmacy. It was located on Front Street, now Kanawha Boulevard, in the block below Capitol Street. Three generations of the Rogers family's ownership ended in 1907 when the business was purchased by Mr. T. B. Stalnaker. Completing 130 years of unbroken service, the original Rogers Drug Store was the oldest in West Virginia. —Dayton, Pioneers & Their Homes on Upper Kanawha, *p. 232*

I did not mention that Norris Whittaker was running a large brick yard of pressed bricks and had several hired hands, mostly Negroes. It was hard work in some ways. One man had to sit up on the kiln to catch the bricks as they were thrown up to be nicely placed inside ready to burn. He must have thought it hard work, as one day while down to his dinner he deliberately took an axe and cut off his right hand.

Poor fellow, how sorry I was for him. He was sent home and I do not know that he was ever punished for it.

Uncle Norris was not a hard master, he did not own any slaves himself. His parents came here from New York State when he was nearly grown. He was always good and kind to me.

Norris S. Whittaker was born in Charleston in 1807, the son of William and Philena (Cobb) Whittaker. His father was a young fur trader from Massachusetts who first came to the valley with Isaac Noyes. Norris Whittaker was a builder and built many of Charleston's best residences, two of which were the Rand and the MacFarland (Ruby) houses. He had first spent a few years as a keel and flat boatman, but he soon followed the family precedent and learned carpentry, brick-making, painting, and every other trade related to building. He was a man of tremendous physical strength and endurance. He was a champion for the cause of temperance, for which it is said he made hundreds of speeches. He was also a strong union man and was appointed postmaster of Charleston during the difficult period of the Civil War. In 1832 Mr. Whittaker married Leticia Morris, daughter of Carroll, a son of Major William Morris. —Dayton, Pioneers & Their Homes on the Upper Kanawha, p. 25.

One day they sent to the school for me to come. I found my Aunt Martha Capehart and my cousin Mary Ann on their way up the river to my father's. As their visit was mostly to see me, they took me with them and that was the last of my schooling in Charleston. My aunt soon found out that I had been neglected in every way. My hair was never combed as I was too young to do it as it should be. She directed my step-mother's attention to it, who found it in an awful condition and it had to be all cut off. Of course I never went back.

This was in 1836 and I was now eight years old, Father said he would not board me from home any more without it would be with one of my aunts at Coalsmouth.

My step-mother had her sister Kitty Morris

McFarland House, 1310 Kanawha Boulevard, Charleston. Built in 1836 by Norris Whittaker, it is one of the valley's oldest and most significant homes. Used as a hospital during the war, the house is now a private residence. It received several direct artillery hits in the 1862 campaign. COURTESY ELIZABETH HUBBARD, RAC

living with her at this time. My half-brother Carroll was a very delicate child so small that they gave him the nickname of "Kitten" that he still goes by and very few people know his right name. He was the baby and very sick when my aunt was there. So she took me home with her to Coalsmouth to go to school to Uncle Joe Capehart, her husband.

I do not remember much about that school except one thing. It was about "pantilets" something like drawers, except they were tied on each leg with garters at the knee and they had to come down over the top of the shoes. They were always elaborately trimmed with lace, as our dresses came half way between the knee and the shoe. I had to wear them and no one else in school had to. I had come from Charleston where they were fashiosnable but they had not yet reached the country. Therefore I was the laughing stock of the school and this made me so unhappy. As I would go to school through the creek bottom, a thick wood at that time, I would take my "pantilets" off and hide them under a log until I came back in the evening. My aunt found out and would never make me wear them again until I started back home. She said she thought it foolish for my step-mother to insist on me wearing them there in the country where no one else had them. So this was the only sorrow I had while there. Of course they all petted me for my mother's sake if nothing else.

This was the last of my boarding from home. When I went back home a Mr. Pryor was teaching on the opposite side of the river. Father would take me in the morning and come for me in the evening. But one evening I came to the landing and found the canoe was on my side. Father stood on the other side calling to me to get in and take the paddle and said I could come over safely. It never entered my mind not to obey him nor did I feel fear when he was there. Although I had never paddled a canoe in my life, I jumped in, took the paddle and did just as he told me and came over safely. The canoe was very small and light.

ABOUT THIS TIME another one of my stepmother's sisters came to stay awhile, she was a widow with two children and her name was Parthenia Greenlee. Her oldest child was a daughter about my age, named Maria. She was pretty and very bright and of course a favorite with her two aunts, my step-mother and Aunt Kitty. They would help her with her lessons and hear her pieces. In those days we all had to learn long pieces of poetry by heart to say every Friday. She could always rattle hers off without missing a word, she had so much confidence in herself. But I was so timid and frightened at even a cross look that I could never say all of mine. Aunt Kitty was the only one except my father that would teach me and have patience with me. That was an unhappy year for me as I was always put in the background while my cousin was held up as a prodigy of all that was smart and good. It got so even Father thought I was dull and did not like my books. My step-mother would say "Mary Jane you get your knitting, no use to waste your time over your books, you will never learn. Maria you take the book and read."

They left there and some years after Mrs. Greenlee went to Missouri and there married again, a Mr. Everette. One of her daughters by her last husband married a Mr. G. Staton and they are now living on a farm just below Red House and have a large family.

About this time (1837) there was a Miss Sarah Kiger who came to Paint Creek to teach a young ladies school and my Aunt Kitty and myself attended. Aunt Kitty was grown and I was about nine years old. She had quite a large school, all of Uncle Felix Hansford's girls went, Pattie, Sallie and Bettie.

Miss Kiger boarded at Uncle Felixes and taught school in Uncle Carroll Hansford's house which was just across Paint Creek. It was a three-story frame house built against the face of the mountain and bolted to solid rock. We went up steps on the side of the mountain at the end of the house and went in the third story from the front, where the school was taught. My uncle had a store in the lower rooms that looked out on the road with a large portico in front and a pretty yard set with evergreens, holly, spruce and pine.

Uncle Carroll was very industrious always busy and he thought a great deal of his home. He was a young man at that time and was in love with our school teacher, so the old people said, and it was thought at one time they would marry.

Miss Sarah Kiger taught common English branches and painting with water colors. Flowers were cut out of heavy oil paper, placed over cardboard and painted with large stiff brushes. All the older girls took lessons, I was anxious to learn to paint, but I was too young, they said.

I wanted to learn to draw but Miss Sarah knew nothing about that. So my father bought me a small box of children's paints and also a long red pencil. I thought so much of my pencil as they were not common at that time. Every girl in school wanted to borrow it. One day it disappeared and some of the girls said a certain one had it. I asked everyone and no one had seen it. I asked the teacher for permission to search out doors. After I had looked every place I knelt down beside the building and prayed to God to show me where my pencil was. Just as I arose from my knees it dropped down before me. I suppose it had been about my clothes and my prayers were answered. Oh, what firm childish faith I had then. I always took my little troubles to God, but that is the only time I remember having my prayers answered immediately.

I went to school all that winter, it was the coldest weather. I was always dressed warmly in a heavy linsey dress with long sleeve gingham aprons, heavy leather shoes and yarn stockings. I remember one day in March there was a very deep snow, and the night before it had sleeted, it was like walking on ice all the way. Father went to school with us, carrying me most of the way.

There was the greatest number of red birds laying on the snow in every direction, some were alive and some were dead. I wanted to pick them all up, Aunt Kitty got some and so did I. When we got to the school house we found all the children had brought some in, so many that the teacher had to object to any more. They were most all dead though, by the time we went home.

In May we had a May Festival up on a high mountain. We children worked hard to fix for it and so did everyone else. Everyone in the neighborhood took the greatest interest in it as it was the first thing of the kind that had ever been held. Aunt Kitty was the Queen of May, cousins Pattie Hansford and Susan Morris were two of the maids of honor. I cannot remember the others. Cousin Bettie Hansford and myself were pages, we walked in front of the queen, strewing flowers. There was a throne of plank covered with moss, and on this was a large arm chair covered with red check. There was an arch above of flowers and evergreens.

The queen and her maids of honor all made speeches. After that there was a long plank table loaded with everything good to eat. All the girls were dressed in white and were bare-headed with wreaths of flowers in their hair.

I remember while I was going to school to Miss Sarah that Aunt Sallie White made a carpet woven of shucks. It was pure white and Miss Sarah painted flowers on it with her Therim paints, it was beautiful.

We lived about a mile below, and between our house and theirs, was a little cabin in which my grandfather's sister, Aunt Sallie White lived. They came from Culpepper County, Virginia. I loved her, she was always so bright and cheerful with some fun for the children in her pocket. I never remember her coming up to our house that she did not bring me something, poor as she was. There are many of her descendants still living in Kanawha. Her eldest grand-daughter married a Mr. Trimble.

Aunt Sallie was one of the kindest persons to children. I always loved to stay there, Bettie and myself were the best of friends. Aunt Sallie was very delicate when she first married. She knew nothing about housekeeping and had to leave it all to the Negroes, or at least one woman, Nelly, who was a splendid hand in every way. However Aunt Sallie lived to be 94.

Grandfather Hansford was sent to the General Assembly of Virginia from Kanawha County for 17 consecutive years (1811–1818). Sometime before this he had built a church, or a meeting house as it was then called, on his place just below the garden. It was about where the Crown Hill Coal Company store now stands. It was a Baptist church and had a meeting once a month.

O H, WHAT HAPPY TIMES the people seemed to have, I was only a child but I can remember seeing them shouting and shaking hands. The lower end of the church was for the Negroes, there was a side door and they always came in and took their seats when the white people did. They always seemed to enjoy it as much or more as anybody.

As it was about two miles from where we lived, we always went down in a canoe and stayed to dinner at Grandfathers. They usually made preparations for a large crowd on preaching day. I always looked forward to this as the happiest times of my life.

Grandfather had a good many colored people. So many little children that I played with. The little Negroes were my best playmates for they were better behaved than half of the children now. I never heard an improper word such as swearing and they were taught from infancy not to fight or strike a white child.

How I remember the cook, old Aunt Lucy. We were always taught to call all grown Negroes Uncle or Aunt out of respect, and we were never allowed to talk back or disobey an auntie any more than our mother. Aunt Lucy was as black as coal, shining face and white cap with a broad ruffle that set off her smiling black face.

She always had something good for me. She was the wife of Grandfather's shoe maker who made shoes for both white and black. It kept him busy the year around and his name was Basil. Grandfather also had a blacksmith and teamster, that did nothing else. I have forgotten how many men he had in all.

William Henry Edwards, born in 1822 in New York, became interested in surveying coal in the Kanawha Valley and acquired thousands of acres of coal lands along Paint Creek in the late 1840s. He settled in Coalburg and opened his first mine in 1853, later becoming the president of the Ohio and Kanawha Coal Company. Edwards was also interested in scientific and literary pursuits. SWV

Grandmother had a seamstress named Bettie that stayed always in her room cutting and sewing for both black and white. Sindy was the weaver, Pat was the house maid and Eliza waited on Grandmother in her room. She was an invalid for a long time. Besides there was ever so many little fellows always around waiting on their mothers.

I have forgotten who attended to the milk but I know they always had plenty kept in one of the nicest stone milk houses in one corner of the yard. Water was brought in by wooden pipes to stone troughs at the door, from a large spring on the mountain. It was also brought in wooden pipes to the barnyard into wooden troughs, where all the stock was watered.

*Major Hansford was a prominent man in the valley in the early years of the 19th century, and as distinguished in his appearance and person-*ality as he was prominent. He operated several salt furnaces and cultivated his many acres of farm land with his slaves, to whom he would tolerate no mistreatment.

Col. William H. Edwards, 1822–1909, was one of the valley's first coal operators. In 1849, while on one of his trips to the Kanawha, made the following entry in his Journal:

"One day I was passing John Hansford's house on my way back from Cabin Creek, when Mr. Hansford called to me from the porch of his house to come up. I went in and he entertained me for some time telling of his early years in the Kanawha Valley. Several times he had barely escaped with his life from Indians. He pointed to a pear tree on the river bottom below his house and said that his original cabin had stood beside that tree, and many times he had stood guard with his rifle while his wife milked the cow, to protect her form the Indians.

"Mr. Hansford had represented Kanawha County in the Legislature several times in the early part of the century. He used to ride his horse to Richmond and ride home again at the end of the term. The road that passed his house used to be the only thoroughfare between Kentucky, Richmond, and Washington, and Henry Clay and other Senators and members of Congress used to pass that way and put up at his house. He told of Chief Justice Marshall (when a young man) coming to the region on land business, and especially Albert Gallatin (Secretary of the Treasury 1808–1813) who about 1794 took up many tracts of land along the Kanawha River.

"He died soon after I saw him. Mrs. Hansfod survived him half a dozen years. She was bedridden, and had been for several years, but her mind was bright and she liked to see people and talk. She was a daughter of William Morris, and had been brought from the east of Virginia on horseback by her father when she was almost a baby." Memoirs of William H. Edwards.

Grandfather was looked up to as one of the great men of the neighborhood. He was not what you would call wealthy but they certainly did have everything to make them comfortable and happy. He had a beautiful terraced garden with nice cut stone steps from one level to another. That garden was my delight. All kinds of flowers including the sweet old fashioned annuals.

Major John Hansford's house, the first frame house in the Kanawha Valley, was built at present crown hill in 1795. WVSA

There was also filbert bushes with a large pecan tree and a walnut tree in the front yard. There was also plenty of walnut and chestnut trees just back of the house on the mountain. They had small fruit trees of all kinds and one of the largest pear trees I ever saw, down in the field some distance from the house. I can remember going in a wagon with the Negroes to get the pears.

At the time Grandfather had five married sons all living around him. Uncle Felix had built himself a nice brick house near the mouth of Paint Creek and on the public road. Uncle Milton lived at my Father's old home up the creek at the mill. Uncle Galliton lived just below the meeting house in a nice little white cottage built by Uncle Marshall. Uncle Morris Hansford lived on the James River and Kanawha Turnpike and kept a toll gate just opposite to what is now called Clifton or Dego. After he returned from Missouri he built himself a cottage and also a storehouse on the side of the hill. There was a stone wall from the road up, forming a terrace in front looking down on the toll gate. There was just room for the road between the house and the river. It looked wild and remote yet it was a rather public place as there was a ferry kept here as far back as I can remember. It had a large boat for all kinds of vehicles.

I believe I said Uncle Morris married Cousin Kitty Morris, her mother was a Miss Barnes. I cannot remember whether it was her mother's father or brother that was the first inventor of the steam boat, and tried to run it on the Potomac. She had many letters from him while he was in London trying to get some help. She was living with Uncle Morris when I was young and we all called her Aunt Polly. I used to love to go to her room and hear her talk. Uncle Morris had built her a room to herself in the yard and her unmarried daughter Jannette Morris lived with them and kept house for her sister Kitty. They had three children, all boys; William, Monroe and Frank.

Mollie Hansford's great uncle William Morris III who was sent to the Legislature in 1796 and attended William and Mary College, married Polly Barnes. Her mother was a sister of James Rumsey, the inventor of the steam boat. Polly Barnes' father, Joseph Barnes was a carpenter and made the boats for Rumsey. Rumsey went to Europe to gain support for his invention but

In 1839, Stockton's Inn opened its doors to visiting stagecoaches at Kanawha Falls on the James River and Kanawha Turnpike. The Inn was owned by Col. Aaron Stockton, a slave-owning farmer and coal entrepreneur. The central unit is the original section of the building, with the wings added after the Civil War. Thousands of troops passed by here during the war and in the fall of 1861 Federal forces used it as a quartermaster depot. In November 1861 Confederates fired at the house from the heights of Cotton Hill. The Inn, called the Glen Ferris Inn since 1929, is owned by Elkem Co. and is on the National Register of Historic Places.

It was a sad time when Father came home with the news that it was decided against him. All I heard him say was that Stockton was a "Grand Rascal." He said he had bribed witnesses to swear falsely that they knew nothing about the land in any way. One was a man that lived near us but we had never had anything to do with the family as they were a low degraded set. My stepmother seemed to take it harder than Father, I know now as I can remember how she talked.

died in London in 1791. It is said that after Rumsey's death, Joseph Barnes went to London to take care of his brother-in-law's affairs and was never more heard from. —W. Va. Historical Mag., Vol. 3, 1903, p. 189.

About this time old Col. Stockton had bought some of the land that belonged to my father's grandfather, William Morris. It adjoined our place and he brought suit in regard to the line between them. He claimed enough to take in our house.

Stockton was a gambler by profession, what was then called a "black leg." He spent his winters in New Orleans and the summers at White Sulphur, which was a great resort for all the rich planters from the south. His wife lived at the old Morris house and kept a tavern. I learned all this as I grew up. I only remember seeing old Stockton once, coming to the post office. My father kept it at that time in his store and the name of the post office was Hansford.

Since I am grown now and look back I think Stockton wished to get Father away from there. He knew if he took in his house which was close to the line, Father would sell out and leave.

Aaron Stockton was born in 1776 in New Jersey. He came to Kentucky where he married Elizabeth Tompkins, sister of William Tompkins of "Cedar Grove." After serving in the War of 1812 he removed to the Kanawha Valley about 1815. He and his brother-in-law, William Tompkins, became active in the salt business. About 1827 Stockton became identified with the Kanawha Falls locality where he operated a saw mill, ran a ferry, and was proprietor of a well-known tavern popular with stage coach passengers.

Col. William H. Edwards stopped at the tavern quite often and took the time to write a brief biography of Stockton:

"Mrs. Stockton kept a comfortable house of entertainment and I was always glad to reach it in my travels. Her husband, Aaron, was a character. He was a cousin of Commodore Robert F. Stockton, the noted Naval Commander. He was a man of resources and energy but at the same time he was a gambler, reckless in all his activities, quarrelsome and litigious. He was liked, however, by most of his neighbors. He ran through most of his property and lived at his wife's boarding house, encumbered with debts which he did not trouble his head about." —Memoirs of Col. William H. Edwards.

Tᴴᴱʸ ᴄᴏɴᴄʟᴜᴅᴇᴅ ᴛᴏ ᴍᴏᴠᴇ to Coalsmouth and rented the large tavern house from my Uncle James Teays. This was the fall of 1839 and we moved in a large flat boat. It had a good top and two rooms large enough to hold all our furniture and also all of our colored people. There was Aunt Tildy and her children, Lucy, Nelly, Tildy, Hannah and Wesley. There was also my girl Jane and the man Grandfather gave my father, named Nick. Aunt Tildy's husband Frank Bowles was a free Negro but he lived with us. He went down by land to take the horses and cows.

My step-mother and the two youngest children, Carroll and Victoria, a baby just a little over a year old, stopped in Charleston at her sister's, Mrs. Whittaker. Father, Charley and myself came on the boat and it was very cold and disagreeable. The wind blew so hard that we had to land and tie up a few miles below Charleston at Mr. McMullen's landing. I remember the snow was very deep and Father took us children up to the house where we got supper and stayed all night. Mr. McMullen had a daughter about my age and of the same name, Mary Jane, and we had a great time playing that night. I never saw her again until after we were both grown. She became Mrs. Elliot Hudson and came to St. Albans to live.

We arrived at Coalsmouth the next evening and we children with Father left the boat and went to Uncle John Capehart's to stay all night. The next morning the river was frozen over at the mouth and our boat was fast for some time. The Negroes stayed on the boat as Father found out he could not get possession of the tavern house he had rented. A Mr. Charles Carter was in it and would not give it up until his time was out, which would be two more months.

We arrived at Coal a day or two before Christmas. Mr. Carter had a large family and good many Negroes. He was from old Virginia and had been in possession of the house for several years. The best Father could do was to rent a house from Uncle Joe Capehart. It was a large square brick house near the mouth of Tacketts Creek on the land that came by Aunt Martha. The house was not near finished, only two rooms that were comfortable. They had good Negro cabins and other necessary houses so we were moved into the house by the time Mother and

Flatboats carried animals and produce down the western rivers. Since this was the only cheap means of transportation, the rivers were vitally important. ᴡᴠᴜ

Aunt Kitty came. I stayed with my aunts while Father was getting the house ready, trying to make it more habitable. To look at it on the outside you would think it a fine house. It had large fancy windows in front and a very large door with glass above and on each side and it entered into a very large hall equal to a room. It was on a beautiful situation with a large lawn sloping down to the river. There was no road in front on the river bank like there is now.

According to tradition passed down through some of the older St. Albans families, this house was practically destroyed by fire some time before the Civil War. The foundation and possibly some of the walls were salvaged and it was rebuilt almost as it was before. It was known as the John Hansford house and is still standing below the railroad bridge and near the mouth of Tackets Creek.

During the Civil War, wounded soldiers were brought there after the Battle of Scary. It is said that one soldier was laid in the hallway where the blood from his wounds stained the floor.

Mrs. Elizabeth Green, now living in St. Albans, states that her aunt, Elizabeth Taylor, lived in the house at one time and she often visited there. Mrs. Green could vividly recall the dark brown stain on the hallway floor which she was told was where the soldier had lain. The floor has since been resurfaced and no such stain exists today.

John Hansford House. AC

Since the place has long been known as the John Hansford house, Mollie's father must have moved back in it some time after she married and left home in 1853. He was living there on October 10, 1875, when he was killed by a train, while walking across the railroad trestle, only a few yards from the house. As the railroad was not completed until January 1, 1873, he surely must have been one of the first railroad fatalities in the valley. It could possibly have been John Hansford's body that was laid in the hall after he was hit nearby on the railroad.

Uncle Joe Capehart, instead of finishing this house, built another one on the Pike, near a large spring. There was already a log house there which he weatherboarded and added two or three new rooms to. He also added a nice porch and had water from the spring brought to the house in pipes. He also set out trees but like the other house, he never finished the inside. He never plastered or finished the wood work. The only excuse to be made for him, was that a good carpenter was hard to get and they would only work by the day.

It was his disposition however to be always changing from one thing to another. Sometimes he would farm, sometimes teach school, and in between he clerked in a store. Once he had a large cooper shop and was making salt barrels. He even tried his hand at raising silk worms, was going to make a fortune selling silk.

This was when I was 13 years old in 1841. By then he had moved back to Grandmother's old house which belonged to Aunt Martha. It was a large house and he took one of the lower rooms for his worms. There was a long plank table through the middle of the room on which he would lay out the mulberry leaves to feed the worms. In a few minutes they would be covered and you could hear the worms eating. It was a low constant "tick-tick-tick," until every leaf was gone. Then they would crawl away, up on the walls of the room and the ceiling, which was crossed with large beams like were in old-fashioned houses. Just before they commenced to spin their silk, they became as clear as glass, almost transparent. The little balls, or cocoons they made, were egg-shaped and all white and lemon colored. They were fastened all over the beams and the walls of the room. When they began to come out they were pretty white butterflies. He would let only a few come out, then he would take them all down and scald them to kill the flies. They were then packed in barrels and shipped to a silk factory. As well as I can remember, at that time there was one at Wheeling and several more in other cities. At the factories, the cocoons were cut, carded and spun into a coarse silk that was very strong and equal to flax thread.

I must go back to our family where I left Father fixing up the house. When Mother, Aunt Kitty, and the children came, there was a bed in

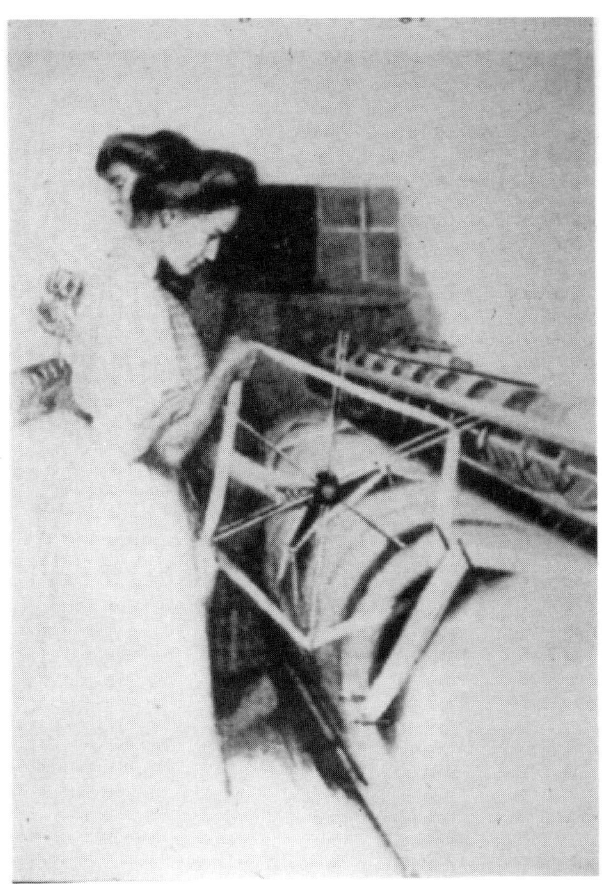

Silk factory in Wheeling, West Virginia. AC

each of the two good rooms, fine high posted curtain bedsteads with a trundle bed to push under. They were comfortable and looked nice and pretty. Aunt Kitty and myself slept in the front room where we entertained any company. Mother and Father and the three children were in the other room.

People of this day and time cannot realize what a convenience a trundle bed was. During the day it was pushed under the large bed and there was always a deep ruffle or valance around the legs so no one could see it. They were as good for a grown up as they were for a child. Nothing half as useful or convenient has been invented since.

There was another convenience, the curtain bed. If you were sick or weary you could lay down on your bed and let down the curtains and you would be as private as if you were in another room. If callers came in, you need not see them if you did not feel like it. I should like to see anything like that now, in two rooms, where you were obliged to entertain company when they came.

I was happy and contented here. Although I was eleven years old I did not look over seven and I was as innocent and ignorant as one of that age. Mother bought me a doll, it was a little wooden one that had joints. I could make it kneel or sit down and devoted much of my time when alone dressing it and washing its clothes. It was the only doll I had ever owned that I was permitted to play with it as I wished. The two wax dolls that I spoke of before that Uncle James Teays and Father gave me were ready dressed, in yellow crepe and pink silk. My step-mother thought them entirely too nice for me to play with and they were set on the mantle piece where I could look at them but could seldom touch. One was named "Mrs Washington Patts," the other for the heroine in a story book.

I was too young to know what the story was about but it was first published in Goodys Magazine when it first came out in the 1830's. Father was postmaster and it first came through the office and then he subscribed for it for many years after. I have a number of them bound that were published in the 1840's.

There were very few persons at that time who took a magazine. I do not remember but one person in Coalsmouth that took one when we did and that was Mr. Lasley. There was plenty of rich men however that could have done so. Father was also postmaster after we came to Coalsmouth, therefore, I knew who took magazines.

Getting back to my dolls, I kept them for years. Mother was right in one way not to let me have them, yet I never did get to enjoy them.

One of the most eaten foods then was frumenty. It was put in a large iron pot that held a half bushel and hung on the crane over the big wood fire and there it would boil all day. At night when it was done, all the children, white and black, would have a bowl full. It was given them with a little salt and plenty of milk over it. This was our supper and then to bed not later than eight o'clock.

I remember one night Aunt Kitty was gone from home for the evening and when she came back I was in bed asleep. There was a little cat that I often played with, curled up on my shoulder with its mouth on my face. She immediately jerked the cat off, waking me up saying the cat

Stewpot, skillet and gridiron by Edwin Tunis. ETFL

was sucking my breath. At that time everyone believed in such things. She quickly took the cat out to the kitchen to get one of the Negroes to kill it. They were all afraid, however, to do it saying "cats would come back and 'hant' you." Negroes were all afraid of what they called hants and ghosts. Aunt Kitty, determined to have the cat killed and took it to Father, who took it out to the wood pile and gave it a stroke with the axe. He thought he had cut its head off, as it was dark. Aunt Kitty came back through the hall and met the cat coming through the front door dragging its head on one side and blood spurting all over. I tell you she hollowed out and ran back out. All the Negroes were there in a minute to see what had happened. They were saying "I told you so," and no one could convince them that it was not a ghost, especially since it was found dead later.

I wish the Negroes were as happy and comfortable now as they were then. Every night they would sing hymns and seemed to enjoy them, they all had splendid voices.

Jane always slept in our room that she might be there if the children needed her. In the morning she got up and made the fire, cleaned up our room and set the table while Lucy dressed the children. Our breakfast was most always fried pork or sausage, fried hominy, coffee and corn bread with molasses and butter. We had wheat bread if we had company. The Negroes had the same thing except the coffee and corn bread.

Father always clothed his people well. I never remember seeing any of them ragged or dirty, the women always kept all the clothes mended and clean. Aunt Tildia sewed as she did not have the cooking to do. At that time our man Nick was a good cook. Mother had taught him when we kept the stage stop at Paint Creek. I can see him now broiling a steak on an old-fashioned grid iron made of round crossed bars. This was set on a bed of live coals, wood of course. Then he would turn the steak with his long fork and lift it out into a dish of butter, with the red juice streaming out into the dish. I have never tasted a steak equal to it since.

Then he had a pair of waffle irons with handles three feet long that opened and shut like tongs. He would pour in the batter then thrust the irons into the big wood fire, turn them over and pull them out as fast as you can bake griddle cakes now. They would come out golden brown and were buttered immediately. How delicious, there is no bread now to equal them. The corn bread was the same, there is none today that can taste as sweet as it did then. It was made up in a large wooden tray with cold water, the colder the better. Add a little salt and when the dough was stiff enough you took it up in your hands and made it into small pones. they were placed in rows in a dutch oven with a tight lid. Coals of fire were then heaped on and under it and on a wide hearth it would bake slowly.

When they roasted a turkey, it was put in what we called a "reflector or tin kitchen." A large deep tin pan set on legs and closed up at both ends back and top leaving one side open to the fire. The turkey was put on a spit and it was set before the fire. Then it was turned, basted and turned carefully not to cook too fast. I tell you they were roasted nice and sweet.

I remember all this as I was in the kitchen a great part of my time playing with the little Negroes. I could knit very well and knitted socks and stockings for the children.

I used to go to the post office with Aunt Kitty. She went regularly as she had a beau in Charleston that she corresponded with and she got one letter every week. There was only a foot path up the bank of Coal River where Tacketts Creek emptied into Coal. There was a long trestle that reached across. At first we were afraid to cross without someone leading us. We soon got so we could almost run across.

The ladies at that time wore short dresses that came to the ankle showing the low-quartered shoes and white stockings. Aunt Kitty's feet always looked nice, she prided herself on her pretty feet. Although the mud was deep she could walk without getting any or very little on her shoes. I remember this, as she lectured me on keeping my feet nice and told me of the compliments paid her on her feet.

In those days young ladies never went any place alone. If they had no company they would always take one of the servants. That was the reason I always got to go with Aunt Kitty. She was always kind and taught me everything I knew about sewing. She taught me drawn work or hemstitching as they called it then.

The other children took up all of my stepmother's time. Charley was her pet and idol. If she bought anything valuable she would say that was for Charley. I remember when they bought the silver spoon and the big ladle, she said the ladle was to be for him, she also got him fine books. Charley was very bright and full of life and good humor, for everyone spoiled him. Carroll was the reverse, he never had much to say and would never go where there was company. Carroll would stay with me or Lucy the nurse, for hours playing by himself, while Charley would be entertaining company. He was easily frightened and would wake up screaming and could not be quieted. Father was the only

Teays Tavern at Coalsmouth. WVS

one who could quiet him. He would take him up in his arms and sing to him. This continued until he was a large boy. After his mother's death I always felt sorry for him. He was the baby when Victoria came and of course she took his place. Being such a quiet sad child he did not get the attention he should have had, it was not calculated to brighten him up.

I know by experience for I was the same. I never had anyone to kiss me or tell me they loved me or petted me in any way. Therefore, I was always silent and shy and undemonstrative. I might love someone ever so much but I never thought of showing it. This has clung to me all my life and I think it was the same way with Carroll. I know he had an affectionate disposition when a child, but like me he had nothing to bring it out. If you are loving and affectionate to a child he will naturally be so in return.

The house we were living in was the only house between the mouth of Coal River and the bridge on the lower side. There was a nice brick house however on the upper side almost opposite. It was built by a man named Angel and was burned down during the war. Mr. Vickers' house was just where it is now, one of the oldest houses in that vicinity.

In March, Father moved to the tavern house at the bridge and Mr. Carter moved into the house we left. Father bought a good many pieces of furniture from him. He bought a fine side board, a set of chairs and bedsteads that he could not move to the house he was going to.

This tavern house was built by Mollie Hansford's uncle, James T. Teays in 1831. It was a large six-room, two-story frame house which was later enlarged to twelve rooms. It was located on the lower side of Coal River on the James River and Kanawha Turnpike. In 1832, James Teays and Col. Philip Thompson built a toll bridge at that point and the tavern became a stopping place for the four-horse stages. Not only was it an exchange point for the horses, there was a toll gate there and practically everyone who traveled the road stopped at the tavern house. It was used as a hotel until 1876 and then as a residence by the Teays and Barker families until the 1930's. Callahans Centennial History of W. Va.; W. Va. Historical Magazine, 1903; Coalsmouth Journal, Vol. 1, No. 4. (See front cover.)

The first school in Coalsmouth was started in this house in 1827. It was for girls only and the teacher was Eliza Fry, a daughter of Phillip R. Thompson. It is the oldest house in St. Albans, built before 1818, and is still in use.

Soon after we moved, I commenced going to school to a Mr. Waldon who taught in the big log church. It was the only church and schoolhouse near Coalsmouth. My Grandmother Teays gave the land and helped build the church. It was free to all denominations but was considered a Methodist church as there were very few other denominations around. Uncle James Teays carried on a Sunday School there until he moved west. It was a large square log house with four windows, two in front and one on each end. There was one large door opposite the pulpit. There were several steps and a wide platform in front of the pulpit. There was a table always there with a pitcher of water and a glass on it during preaching. You would see women getting up and taking children up to get water in the summer time. I have often seen women take their babies up and lay them on the platform to sleep.

Children were always brought to church at that time by those who had no servants to leave them with. I have often seen a mother and father with five or six children all come in together. By the way, men went to church in those days. It was considered very low and ungenteel to be seen standing around loafing any place during church. I must say however that many came that did not come in until the sermon was over.

The church made a comfortable school house as it was large and the benches were comfortable. There was a long table against the wall at one end where we all had to write and where our copy books, pen and ink were kept. We used quill pens, we brought the goose quills to school and the teacher made them. I never saw a steel pen until after I quit going to school. There was no such thing as a black board. There was great pains taken with little children learning to write

much more than there is at this time. The church was surrounded by beautiful large trees, mostly beech, that afforded plenty of shade and limbs for swings. The yard was large and sloped down to Tackets Creek at the back, with the county road in front.

I did not go very long to Mr. Waldon as he drank and it broke up his school. After that I went to Mr. Redmond Rust and Aunt Kitty, but I have forgotten which one taught first. All I remember about Aunt Kitty's school was that she undertook to whip Cousin Steve Capehart who was about ten years old and she could not manage it. She had to call on Cousin Lizzie Thomas and me to hold him for her. Cousin Lizzie would not do it, but I had been taught to obey her in everything. Although it almost killed me to do so, I went up and took hold of him in a very feeble way. She called up someone else but after it was all over Steve said, "I would not have given up but I feared she would whip Mollie," (me). Of course I felt mean but they all seemed to understand it.

What I remember most about Mr. Rust's school was he was walking up and down with his long switch in his hand. He had told us to study and get ready for our lessons. Cousin Bettie Wilson, now Chilton, and me were sitting together whispering and did not mind what he had said and went on whispering. He came up behind us and gave us several cuts with the

Birkett Davenport Fry, one of Eliza Fry's sons, was born in the school house in 1822. He attended West Point and became a Confederate General during the Civil War. *ST. ALBANS HISTORY, 1993, SAH*

switch. I was so mortified I cried and Cousin Bettie was so mad she quit school for some time. She at last came back but she never forgave him and she would throw it up to him after she was grown, so he told me long years after. I never thought of it again as I was only twelve years old at the time.

He was ten years and eight months older and I looked on him as I would a father and I liked and respected him. Although he was very strict in school yet he was very kind and used to often give me a large russet apple. I thought that no one else had that kind of apples as his name was Rust and I thought they were Rust apples.

I married him many years after when I was a widow and he a widower. I found him to be one of the best of men, the most patient, kind and considerate beings in the world. He has often told me that he never thought of me as a child going to school. He remembered how I used to come leading Charley by the hand, lifting him over all the mud holes and carrying his book,

taking off his hat and hanging it up. Then how at recess I would wash his face and smooth his hair in such an efficient matter-of-fact way, as if I was grown. He said he often noticed what a thoughtful child I was and imagined that I would make someone a good wife.

Little did we think how it would be and our lives would be spent together in happiness and contentment as if the Heavenly Father had directed it all.

I remember going with Aunt Kitty to get her school started. There was no such thing as free schools in Kanawha County. It took a paper drawn up in good form for anyone who wished to send their children to her. They had to put the names down of how many they would send.

I liked to go with her and see and hear the different people. Some were funny and some could not read. Aunt Kitty would generally use them as object lessons to me that I never forgot. I expect she did not remember them an hour after.

This school was of a type known as "Old Field Schools." The name came from the practice of usually building the school house in some old abandoned field not used for cultivation.

In autumn a stranger would appear on the scene and the report would go around that there was a "school-master" in the neighborhood. From whence he came none knew. He brought no credentials or a diploma from a college faculty, for none was required; it was only necessary that he be able to teach the three R's—reading, riting, and rithmetic. To teach these he would bind himself in his "article," which he carried from house to house, soliciting subscribers to the school. Then he would go to the overseer of the poor who agreed in compliance with the law of 1796, to pay the tuition for the indigent children of the neighborhood.

When all was in readiness for the first day, a stentorian voice from the door would cry out, "Come in to books." In they would go with their lunch in a split hickory basket and an "English Reader" and "Websters Speller" under their arms. When the term closed, the teacher made his collection and went, often none knew where.

Such were the pioneer schools of the Kanawha Valley before the "Free School System of 1846." —History of the Great Kanawha

Felix Hansford house built at the mouth of Paint Creek in 1825. Still standing in 1996. PHC

Valley by John P. Hale and Virgil A. Lewis, 1891.

Cousin John Teays, the father of Cousin Tom that married my sister Vicky, lived at that time where Cousin James Teays now lives and carried on a large tan yard. It was just back of the house between them and the creek. It always looked cheerful and lively there as he had several hired hands. There would be several wagon loads of tan bark coming in and loads of hides. Cousin John was a very industrious man and seemed to me to be one of the best men, so patient and quiet. I remember thinking so and liking him although I saw very little of him as he was always at work. His wife, Cousin Malinda, was just the reverse. He married her in Monroe County. She was very fond of dress and although she had several children she dressed like a young girl, so I would hear my aunts say. That was not exactly true as she always wore a fine lace cap covered with bows of colored ribbon. She had her hair puffed on side combs in front of the

cap. Most married ladies wore caps then.

When Uncle John Capehart was married, Aunt Kitty and I went to the wedding and everyone said Cousin Malinda was the best dressed lady there. I remember her dress, it was a delicate lemon color and it was trimmed with white satin piping and blond lace. It was a fine silk lace that we never see now but it was beautiful. Her dress was made very much as they do now, wide skirt, plain waist with capes over the shoulders.

We were all invited to Uncle John's to the infare or reception, the next day. Mother wore a black silk that she had bought in Charleston, on her way down. She also wore a fine shawl, black with red and green figures all over it. Aunt Kitty had a small white merino shawl with embroidered flowers in the corner, and I had a red one the same. I wore a calico dress that was 37½ cents a yard, it was tea green and I thought it was very fine.

My two aunts, Martha Capehart and Aunt Thenie, always dressed very plainly, although

Dr. and Mollie Walls lived in this house during the Civil War. It is located at Stephen City (was Newtown), seven miles south of Winchester. Still standing in 1996. AC

they were both young and pretty. They were very domestic and visited so little. But they were great hands to go to church and to entertain the preachers.

We had lots of custom travelers going and coming. Father hired out some of the servants. He hired Nick to Mr. Wells living at the Licks, as a cook at his hotel. Lucy was hired to Uncle John Capehart. Jane had begun to learn to cook and she afterwards became our main cook. Nellie was house girl and Hannah and Tildy played with us children.

I do not remember if it was forty-two or three that my step-mother died. She came to breakfast one morning with her upper lip very much swollen. She said it came from a large mole on her lip that she had picked with a pin. No one seemed to think anything of it but it continued to swell all over her face. Dr. Smith of Charleston looked at it and did not seem to know what was the matter. I do not know if Dr. Smith was sent for or just happened to call. She never went to bed as I remember and I know now that it was blood poison from picking the mole. One side of her face and lip mortified. I can see her now sitting in her rocking chair picking pieces of flesh out of the inside.

It was a beautiful evening and the others had all gone in to supper leaving me with her. I was sitting in the back door and she was in her chair as usual. She called me to her and took my hand and said, "Mary Jane I will soon leave you all and I want you to promise me to be good to my children. Maybe Kitty will not be here long and I know I have not treated you as I should have." Then she repeated it "be good to my children." I never answered as I was distressed and frightened. She then told me to call the rest of the family and asked them to lay her on the bed. She then asked them to send for Uncle James Teays, that she wanted him to pray and sing. He soon came as he lived just opposite, across the river. She requested him to sing "How Firm a Foundation Ye Saints of the Lord." She then kissed the children and I took them away to bed. She died that night and she was the first person buried in what is now known as Teays Cemetery.

Maria (Morris) Hansford died April 16, 1841, the same year her youngest child was born. Although Mollie Hansford was only twelve years old at the time, she was left with much of the responsibility of the care of her small step-brothers and sisters. —Hansford Family Bible; W. Va. Hist. Mag., July 1903, p. 293.

Oh, it was a sad time, I can remember Aunt Leuticia Whittaker coming down and the baby "Cint" crying. Of course no one noticed me or asked me any questions. Being a very quiet child I never mentioned what Mother said to me. Not even to Aunt Kitty, but I never forgot it. I always tried to be good to the children as near as I knew how. I can see now I might have been more affectionate but as I said before, no one had ever caressed or petted me. I did not know how to throw my arms around one's neck and kiss and hug them and tell them I loved them. If I was not demonstrative, it was not my fault.

I sewed for them and combed their heads and kept them as neat as I could, even before Aunt Kitty got married and left us.

At night we children, both black and white, would sit around the big wood fire and I would tell them stories. Our big dog "Rowl" would get in the ring and seemed to listen as interested as the children. We were all devoted to him as he used to come to meet us as we came from school.

Whenever there was a rise in Coal River there would be a great crowd of boatmen at our house as it was the only hotel near there. Many times we would have 50 or 60 men to supper. They had to bring the boats out over the falls when the water was very high. Many times these boats would be broken apart and sometimes men would be drowned. There was then a great deal of lumber brought down Coal. That is the way people lived up there long before coal was found at Peytona, it kept everyone busy.

They were fed fried meat, biscuits and coffee and they did not care for anything else. Father was very particular that Aunt Kitty or myself should not come in the dining room, nor did he allow the men to come into our part of the house. They were an awful rough set although some of them were rich in land and timber.

There was another thing I have not mentioned, it was the hog drovers. At that time they drove thousands of hogs from Kentucky and Ohio through to Virginia. They would start early in the fall and come on till near Christmas. That is the way farmers in the valley sold their corn and got their meat for the winter. Everybody had plenty of hog and hominy.

Stephen Teays, who settled at Coalsmouth in 1800, established a ferry and kept an inn for travel between that point and the Ohio. By 1808 many drovers from Ohio and Kentucky passed over the Kanawha route to find a market for hogs and other live stock. Lewis Summers recorded that the drovers and travelers used nearly all the surplus grain along the route and that many sheep and hogs were destroyed by wolves and bears.

It was estimated that in the fall of 1826, about 60,000 hogs passed up the valley of Kanawha,

Tombstone of Morris Hudson. AC

destined largely to eastern Virginia. This traffic continued until the Civil War and it stimulated the growth of corn among the farmers. It is said that the soil of Teays Valley was worn out by continuous cultivation of corn to supply the demand of hog traffic. Sometimes the drovers greatly interfered with other travel for days at a time. After driving the stock through to Richmond or other eastern cities, they frequently made the return trip on foot. —Callahan's Centennial History of West Virginia, p. 100.

Poor Father; he must have had a hard time in one way after Mother's death as the Negroes did very much as they pleased since I was still a child.

Aunt Kitty had broken off with her beau in Charleston, a Mr. Sam Greenhouse, and she had another one, a young Dr. Sutherland. He was several years younger than she was and the only son of a widowed sister of Mrs. Wilson who was Aunt Thenie's mother-in-law. He was staying at Uncle Sam Wilson's house at that time. His mother lived in Maysville, Kentucky, and

Hog drovers. AC

Graves of Stephen and Mary Teays. AC

used to come up on visits to her sister, Mrs. Wilson. Their maiden names were Bailey and they were cousins to Mr. Redmond Rust, who I married.

There were a great many nice, first-class people living at and near Coalsmsouth at that time. They were the Thompsons, Hudsons, Clarksons, Lewises, Capeharts, Turners, Teays, and Lasleys.

Aunt Kitty used to take me to church up at the Episcopal Church that used to stand above Judge Worth's in what is now called the Hudson Cemetery. It was a small brick church and a Mr. Craze, a minister from Charleston, preached there. She also went to the Presbyterian church at Scary which she belonged to. They had meetings there once a month and Rev. John Brown from Charleston preached at Dr. Merridith's. We rode down on horse-back, left our horses and crossed over the creek in a skiff. He preached at Dr. Merridith's house, people in those days thought nothing of going five or six miles to church.

Just before my step-mother's death there was a Mr. and Mrs. Potter and two children came to our house to board. They were from New York and were fine educated people. They had been living in a house belonging to the widow Fry who was a sister of Col. Thompson's. She had three children, two sons and a daughter. Her daughter married a Mr. Bacon of Richmond. One of her sons, Burket Fry, was educated at West Point and the other, Frank, at Lexington. Mrs. Fry taught school in this house when my mother was a girl and she and my aunts went to

school to her. The house was on what we now know as Cousin Frazier Hansford's farm, half way between the river and the pike and it was a very pretty place.

Mr. Potter came home one Christmas morning on the stage and found his house burning. Of course they did not save much as there was no one home except Mrs. Potter, the cook and two little children. She saved the piano herself by dragging it out the first thing. They also saved what was called a pear glass, a very large looking glass reaching from the floor to the ceiling and setting on short legs. But they did not save any clothes, beds or anything upstairs. Therefore, they had to board until they could get a house and some furniture. I do not know how long they stayed at our house. I only remember that they used to loan Aunt Kitty nice books to read. He had a volume of Shakespeare and used to recite long pieces. It was about this time that Dickens' "Nickelby" was published under the name of Boz. It came out a few chapters at a time and Aunt Kitty used to read it aloud to me. I would tell it to the children in a short and simple way of course. They were as much interested in it as I was. Mr. and Mrs. Potter went to housekeeping in the Episcopal parsonage with what few things they had.

I have forgotten what year Aunt Kitty was married. I know it was in the winter and very cold and she had a large wedding. Aunt Leuticia Whittaker and Uncle Norris came down several days before to help fix for it. Such a time, cooking, baking and making jelly. They had tables set as a cross with a pyramid in the center. The first two levels being boxes covered with white cloth, trimmed with cut paper and cedar and set full of glasses of white and pink jelly. there were oranges and apples between with wax candles in silver candle sticks on each corner. Above this were two or three large cakes with candy interspersed. Then there was a roast pig with an apple in its mouth on one table at the end. At the ends of the other tables there was a roast turkey, a boiled ham, and a roast beef. Then the tables were filled in with every conceivable thing that was good to eat. I looked on in wonder, Uncle Norris and Aunt Luticia attended to it all.

Maria Slaughter, old Mrs. Thompson's niece, was one of Aunt Kitty's bride's maids. Her Aunt Slaughter from New Orleans was there on a visit and had all of her silver with her and she sent it down to them to use on the table. The most beautiful cake baskets, goblets and candle sticks. I thought at the time it was the grandest wedding that ever was or would be again. Aunt Kitty was dressed in white satin.

Cynthia Noyes was one of her bride's maids. Everybody in all the country was invited and most of them were there, good many were from Charleston.

I remember very little about Aunt Kitty after that except she went to Ripley in Jackson County. There they boarded at a hotel and Dr. Sutherland practiced medicine. They did not stay there long, they came back and kept house in the log house on the road coming from the river to the pike. It was where Uncle Wilson and Thenie lived when we moved down to Coal.

I can remember when Cousin Alice was born at Aunt Thenie's at the mouth of the river. I know they told me Aunt Kitty had a little girl. I went down to see her after a few days and thought I must take the baby something so I knitted a little pair of half-hand yarn gloves. I knitted them out of single white yarn with a little green stripe at the top and bottom. When I took them down and gave them to Aunt Kitty I remember how she looked at Aunt Thenie and smiled and thanked me for them. I must have been 15 years old at the time.

Dr. William Bailey Sutherland came to Coalsmouth from Maysville, Kentucky in 1843. Here he married Cathrine F. Morris, daughter of Carroll Morris. His son, Dr. John Hansford Sutherland, married Leah Wilson of St. Albans in 1874. Dr. Sutherland was a physician and druggist, keeping a first-class drug store in St. Albans for many years. —Hardesty's History of Kanawha County.

I ALWAYS HAD A COUGH all the time I was going to school. Sometimes I would have to sit down on the side of the road to cough and rest. No one thought I would ever live to be grown. There was always someone advising Father what to do for me. But he did not believe in dosing. He never gave me anything except at night. If I coughed badly he would come to the bed with a lump of loaf sugar with a few drops of paregoric on it. The rest of the children were as healthy as most children. Vic was a perfect little pine knot, cheeks red as a rose with black hair and eyes, she was very pretty. Cint had light hair, she had a very sore head when she was six or seven years old, some kind of a scalp disease. I know how mad and mortified I was when Aunt Leuticia Whittaker came down to see us once after Aunt Kitty's marriage. She said there was nothing the matter with Cint but neglect and that I had not combed her head, etc. Young as I was, it was as much as I could do not to remind her of how she had neglected me, at the same age, when I boarded with her. How Mother had to cut all my hair off close to my head. Old Aunt Tildy thought it was meant for her and would have said something if she had not been afraid that it would be "sassing" her.

It was a long while getting Cint well, I used to wash it with a soft shaving brush and castile soap and comb what I could every day. She at last had to wear a cap, but after it did get well she had a heavy suit of hair. I think she told me that one time she cut off all her hair and sold it for a big price.

She and Vic both slept with Father when they were little and the two boys slept in the trundle bed. I slept in a single bed, not much larger than a lounge in one corner of the dining room for many years. I coughed so much I could not care for the children. After we moved to the riverside, Cint always slept with me and Vic with Thenie.

My greatest friends and company I had were Mr. Ira Lasley's two daughters Mary and Sallie. They lived just across the bridge opposite to us. We could stand and talk to each other across the river. There was scarcely a day we were not together. They were both younger than I. They had two Negro women, Susan and Hannah. Their kitchen and their house is now standing just as it was then, across the yard apart. On a calm day I could hear Mrs. Lasley call from the back door of the house and give her orders for supper. Everyone had their kitchens far away from the house at that time. Mr. Lasley built that house and they moved into it the same year we moved to the Tavern. They had been living across the Kanawha about where Mohlerville now is. (*Now Nitro*) Mr. Lasley was a school teacher and they came to Kanawha from Louisa

County, Virginia. Mrs. Lasley was such a pleasant good neighbor. She stayed at home all the time. I do not remember but a very few times seeing her even at church. Mr. Lasley kept store after he moved up there. Their cottage had two rooms and I must say that I have spent more pleasant happy days in that house than any other at Coal. They always felt like relations, we always went every place together and read all our books together and always went to the same schools.

About this time there was a Miss America McGinnis from near Barboursville who came to Coal to teach school. She boarded at Uncle Joe Capehart's who by this time had moved back in the brick house that we had lived in at the mouth of Tacketts Creek. She taught in a nice little frame house on the bank of the creek and had a large school. I remember very little about this school except one morning we went in the school house and it was literally covered with caterpillars. Big and little, brown and black, and yellow and striped. There was not just a dozen or so, but there seemed to be hundreds crawling all over the seats, up the walls and on the floors. I remember how I dreaded them. The teacher had them swept out in piles, but never did get entirely rid of them.

She did not teach much longer as she was taken sick. She afterwards married Dr. Maupin of Cabell County. Later she had a brother who came to Coal to practice medicine. She invited Cousin Bettie (Wilson) Chilton and me to pay her a visit the next summer and we went. Brother Charley went with us, he was a little boy then. We went on horseback starting in the morning before sun-up. What a pleasant time we had going over Coal Mountain. The wild grapes were in bloom and the dew was on the ground, the perfume was perfectly delicious.

We stopped at Mr. Alex Handley's for dinner. He had married Miss McGinnis' sister and they lived in Teays Valley on the pike. They were looking for us as Miss Mac (as we called her) had written that we were coming.

We were very tired and worn when we got there, I shall never forget how cordially she received us, even though we had never met her before. What a sweet cool room she gave us, everything so neat. She also had a nice dinner for us and they saw that our horses were attended to. I really have forgotten

if we stayed all night or went on. I know we arrived at Miss McGinnis' late in the evening. We were riding along leisurely singing when we saw Miss Mac coming to meet us.

Alexander Handley was born in Monroe County April 1, 1803 and his parents Samuel and Sarah (Harmon) Handley moved to Putnam County in 1815. (They settled in Teays Valley on land now included in the Sleepy Hollow Golf Course and the old family cemetery is still located on the grounds.) —Hardesty's History of Putnam County, p. 167.

They lived between Guyan and Barboursville. They were comparatively poor as Mr. McGinnis was a farmer with a large family. They lived in what was called a double log house with very large rooms. They used the hall as a dining room. So sweet and cool in the summer, it was June when we were there. Everything was covered with roses all so perfectly neat and sweet. I shall never forget the big pitcher of lemonade on the table.

Edmond McGinnis settled on what was known as the Shelton place between Barboursville and Holderby's Landing (now Huntington) in 1803. William Holderby from York County, Pennsylvania, located at Guyandotte about the same time. Both were assignees of land included in the original Savage grant awarded to soldiers of the French and Indian War.

Dr. Allen McGinnis later built a large brick home in Guyandotte. This house became the headquarters of both Union and Confederate forces during the Civil War. —The Huntington Herald Dispatch, June 25, 1959; Kanawha Valley Leader, Jan. 8, 1960.

WHAT A DELIGHTFUL VISIT I had, as well as can remember Cousin Bettie and Brother Charley only stayed a day or two but I remember of being there three weeks. I know we were invited to Mrs. Holderby's in Barboursville who was an aunt of Miss Mac's. There I became acquainted with their daughter "Sac" as they called her. She was a perfect beauty and had a great many beaus. There was a Mr. Samuels and Dr. Henry Maupin who were both coming to see here at that time. Here parents were very much opposed to Samuels and forbid her seeing him. So he enlisted in an Army regiment then starting for Mexico. He came to bid her farewell while I was there and her mother came to me and asked me not to leave them alone. She then came in at 9 o'clock and told us it was bed time, she looked on us as we were children going to school, so she pretended. We all knew it was to get the gentleman to go, Dr. Maupin was there also. I remember we sang that old song: "Goodbye farewell, farewell, is often heard with a tear, or perhaps with a sigh but give to me when loved ones part, that sweet old word goodbye."

"Sac" did not get to bid Mr. Samuels goodbye and she cried all night. Well, she really went on so that her mother came upstairs and told her that if she would compose herself and go to sleep she could write him a farewell note in the morning before he started. I had my doubts about his getting it.

In 1848 a company was mustered into service at Guyandotte for taking part in the Mexican War. It joined the Army as Co. C, 11th US Infantry at New Orleans and landed with General Scott at Vera Cruz. It took part in the siege of Mexico City and was there at the surrender. The officers commanding the company were Elisha W. McComas, Captain; Wm. W. McComas, First Lieutenant, and Joseph Samuels, Second Lieutenant. Joseph Samuels later became Captain of the Company and remained with the unit until it returned to New York. —Hardesty's History of Cabell Co.; Recollections of Colonel Deweese.

Mrs. Holderby took quite a fancy to me and begged me to stay several weeks with her daughter but I had to come home. A year or two later I heard that "Sac" was married to Dr. Henry Maupin. I never saw her again until they took her to the Insane Asylum at Staunton, Virginia. I saw her on her way home, I think it was in fifty-one. She was at Cousin James Teays' with her uncle. Miss Mac's father had gone on to bring her home. They thought she was so near well. She knew me when I first went in, made a great fuss over me and would have me take a walk with her. She clung to me when I went to start home and begged me to stay all night with her. I consented but Mr.

McGinnis came to me and told me that I would have to be locked up in the room with her if I did stay. I told him I was not afraid and stayed.

I can see her beautiful wild looking eyes now. She would sit up in her bed and look at me and laugh. Sometimes she would tell me she was Henry Clay and sometimes Queen Victoria. I said "Sac" now you lay down and shut your eyes and go to sleep or I will go home and leave you. She would then act like a little child and close her eyes for a second and then call out to me. At last I went to sleep and when I woke in the morning she was up standing in front of the looking glass combing her hair that had been cut off short like a boy's. She turned and said "Mollie you did not know you slept with a boy last night."

That is the last time I ever saw her, but she was sent back to the asylum as incurable and her husband married again. I heard not long ago that she was still there, well and hearty in body but knew no one, not even her mother, who went to see her often.

BUT WHY WRITE all this about a stranger? I must go back to forty-three or four, soon after Aunt Kitty's marriage. Father lost one of his colored men, Nick, who he had hired out. He had been married to a young woman that belonged to Watt Vickers who lived just across the river from us.

He came home one day sick from the "Licks" where he was hired as a cook to Mr. Tom Wells, (the grandfather of Mrs. Sattes), who kept a hotel. Nick always said he was poisoned by another Negro that had been hired there before he was and did not like him getting his place. He was always hanging around the kitchen begging something to eat. One day he came in with a bottle of whiskey and insisted that Nick take a drink. When he went to go he left his bottle and when Nick reminded him of it he said "Oh, I give that to you." He went to take a drink out of it the next day and as he held it up to the light he saw what he took to be a "snake skin." That was a great poison with the Negroes. They very seldom poisoned a white person but often poisoned each other, with very slow poison. They called it "Conjuring" and putting on a "spell."

Nick suffered several months before he died, poor fellow. The night he died old Aunt Tildy

General Edward O. Ord and family. USMHI

came in for me to go out to the cabin, said he was dying and they wanted some of the white folks. I was all there was except Father and the children. So I went, which I should not have done as he suffered so and died screaming. There was an awful storm just when he was dying, I shall never forget that night. Nick's death was a great blow on Father as his loss was a thousand dollars. Besides we all liked Nick and pitied his wife, a young thing named Violet.

Not long after this Jane was married to one of Frank Thompson's colored men named Daniel Whiting. Jane was very young when married. During this time we were getting along the best we could with the children. Father was always good and kind and never scolded or gave me a cross word when I would make woeful mistakes in my sewing. Aunt Tildy complained much of her eyes and put as much on me as she could.

I remember the first jackets, they called them round-a-bouts, that I made for Charley and Carroll. I got the sleeves in upside down and made the "Janes" wrong side out, oh, what a cry I had over them. The first dress I made altogether by myself was a pink calico for myself. I cut it and made it all alone. I wore it to a political ball held up Coal River. There I met Mary Thompson who afterwards became Mrs. General Ord of the U. S. Army.

She was then living with her Grandmother Thompson. I remember her grandmother calling her up and showing her my dress, that I had made, after Father had told her. She also scolded her granddaughter for romping as she had just torn her blue calico dress nearly off on the bushes, and at the same time praising me. Oh, I was very proud and after that I used to try my best to sew well.

Mary Thompson was a daughter of Robert Thompson, son of Philip Roote and Sarah (Slaughter) Thompson of Coalsmouth. Robert

Thompson represented Kanawha County in the Virginia Senate from 1839–1846. Mary Thompson married General Ord and was living in San Antonio, Texas, at the time of his death.

General Edward O. Ord, 1818–1883, was graduated from the U. S. Military Academy in 1839, took part in the Seminole War of Florida, the Mexican War and was engaged in the Indian Wars in the West. In 1861 he was promoted Brigadier-General and given command of the Army of the Potomac. In 1862 he was made Major-General of Volunteers in the Department of Mississippi. General Ord was seriously wounded at Corinth but he was later commanding the forces at the surrender of Vicksburg. He was wounded again at Ft. Harrison but later, while in command of the 10th and 18th Corps, was instrumental in Lee's surrender. After the war, he was subsequently in command of the Dept. of Arkansas, the Dept. of California and the Dept. of Texas.

In 1882, he was appointed Engineer of the Construction of the Mexican Railroad, but died of yellow fever in Cuba on his way home from Vera Cruz. —Appletons' Cyclopaedia of American Biography; Hardesty's History of Kanawha Co.

Mary Thompson Ord, while appearing at a public gathering in Washington with her husband and the Lincolns, became the subject of a public scene of jealous rage by Mary Todd Lincoln.

A little praise is often a great help to one who is trying their best, fault finding is very discouraging. One thing, I always tried to do what I was told and not like some, thinking I knew best. I was always willing to go by older peoples' advice and I now see that is one reason I learned fast and wasted or spoiled very few things.

There is one thing I did that I shall always regret and wished Father and Aunt Kitty had not allowed me to do it. It was using up and destroying my mother's clothes and other little things that my Aunts Martha and Thenie had packed in a trunk and put away for me. If it had never been opened and things taken out and made over for me I suppose I would never have done as I did. When Aunt Kitty was married there was but one dress left and that was silk. The same silk, a half yard deep draped off of the skirt running up in points trimmed in white satin ribbon. A little bow at the top of every point. It certainly was pretty. Aunt Kitty asked me if she might take the ribbon off to tie her wedding tickets with. It was all the fashion at that time to write the tickets and tie them with narrow white ribbon. This was prettier than any she could get and it would save her that much. It was perfectly new, of course, never having been worn but one time. Of course, I told her to take it, never thinking that it was tearing up my mother's wedding dress.

Two other white "jaconette" dresses that she had worked in white linen floss. Very much what is now called Hamburg trimming. There was also a flounce on the skirt and ruffles on the sleeves. They were cut up and made over for me when I went to school in Charleston.

WHEN I CAN FIRST remember the trunk, I used to sit by it and look over all the things. There was a half of cake folded in a napkin, why this was kept I never knew. It was as hard and dry as wood but had no worms or bugs in it. There was a little box with a looking glass in the top. Two pretty little books of poetry and prose, I do not remember their names. A fan that opened and shut; a pair of long white kid gloves that came up to the elbow; a pair of white kid slippers, also a pair of white satin slippers. Both pair were low with pointed toes and with rosettes of satin ribbon. They had steel buckles on top and they also had very high pointed heels that were capped with steel and were no larger than a ten-cent piece at the bottom. I would often try these slippers on with a pair of white silk stockings of hers. At last one day when I tried them on I found that they fit me except I could not stand up on the high heels. We had no heels on shoes at that time, they were perfectly flat and square toes. What do you think I did? I took them out to the kitchen and got Westley to cut them off with the axe. Now was not that dreadful? I then put them on and wore them every day. My mother had a small foot, they were No. 2's.

The beautiful white kid gloves, I cut off and wore out the glove part. I think I made mittens out of the arm parts. In the trunk there was also a large tortis shell comb, one of the prettiest I ever saw. I think they told me it cost fifteen dollars. That I kept until I was grown and had two luck combs made out of it, and I have some pieces yet. My step-mother had a large comb also but not near as large or as pretty.

There were several other things that Father put away for me. One was his miniature painted on ivory in a red Moroco case. There were also two sets of spoons, one set was large table spoons with my mother's name on them. My aunts told me that they were made of silver coin. When grandfather Teays' house burned down he had a box of silver dollars and they were melted but he found them in the ashes in a large lump. He later sent it to the city and had a set of spoons made for each of his daughters. We used those spoons on the table from the time I was a child until I was grown. When I was married I took them with me as they had become thin and cracked across the bowl. I took two that were broken and exchanged them in Winchester for a set of heavy plated spoons that were good for fifteen years. The other four I kept and gave two to Hansford and two to Mamie, thinking they would keep them as heirlooms.

I WAS IN BAD HEALTH and did not think I could live long so I divided what silver I had between them. I had bought a dozen silver forks with my own money, the first year I married Dr. Walls. I bought them of the best silversmith in Baltimore and had my name put on them. They cost thirty dollars and at that time very few persons had silver forks. During the war a Yankee took two when I gave him his dinner. Then af-ter I came back out here I had two more stolen. That left only eight so I gave Hansford four and Mamie four, I suppose they have them now. I am ashamed to say, however,that Mamie took the spoons with her grandmother's name on them and exchanged them for a set of small fashionable tea-spoons, long after she was a married woman. I thought that worse than what I did to mother's clothes, as she knew all about the spoons. It only goes to show how thoughtless young people are.

There is one more thing that I still have and that is my mother's copy book, or at least a book of poetry that she wrote when she went to school. She had no jewelry except a plain gold ring. She was a Methodist and at that day it was against the rules of the church to wear anything of the kind. Not even bows, flowers, or feathers on their bonnets.

I suppose it is foolish of me to regret all these things, if my children do not care, I should not. Everything is changed and no one looks back now. They all go ahead in a rush and I suppose that is best in some ways.

I do not remember very much about Aunt Kitty after her marriage. I know that they kept house in the big log house at the mouth of the lane and what a nice housekeeper she was. When I went to visit her in Barboursville she loaned me her nice "camels hair" riding habit. She would always have everything of the very best. She also loaned me her beautiful silk dress, a light bro-caded heliotrope. I know she moved to Maysville soon after, but I cannot remember the year.

I took music lessons from Mrs. Potter for six months, I used to enjoy going down there and being with her, she was always so gentle and kind.

4

Coming of Age

IT WAS IN '45 when I had my first beau, a young man from old Virginia. He was Mr. Lasley's nephew and he had been to New Orleans and stopped here on his way home. There was a debating society at the old log church and Father and Mr. Lasley would always go and most of the time Mary Lasley and myself would go with them. One evening Mary did not come but this young gentleman came with his uncle and he walked with me. From that night he was always there. The Lasley girls and I were always together, I would go over there in the evening and they taught me to play cards. That was one thing Father never permitted in his house, yet he never forbid me playing.

I was going to school and young Mr. Lasley would often come to meet me and walk home with me and carry my lunch basket. He was young and handsome and a refined gentleman. Of course, I fell in love with him, his delicate attentions of flowers and notes and books captivated me. When he was about starting for home he asked Father if he could write to me and Father told him no because I was too young. Therefore, I did not hear from him except through his letters to his Cousin Mary, in which he would say he would wait and come back in two or three years. However, in about two years he sent a paper with his marriage in it. I shall never forget how I felt.

My next beau was in forty-six, and he was Miss McGinnis' brother Robert. However, I could not bear him, he would write long loving letters. About two years later his brother Dr. Allen McGinnis addressed me.

I spoke of Dr. Allen McGinnis, the brother of Miss McGinnis that taught school there in forty-five. He came to Coal to practice when he first graduated quite young. He boarded with us for a short time. Then Dr. John Thompson took him in partnership with him. Dr. Thompson was the only doctor for twenty miles around Coal. He had a very large practice and everyone liked him. He attended to the poor for nothing and never refused to go when called on.

Dr. John Thompson was the son of Philip R. and Sarah (Slaughter) Thompson. He was born in Culpepper County, Virginia, in 1802 and died at Coalsmouth in 1852. He married Matilda Ann Thornton, daughter of George and Frances B. Thornton. She died in 1833 when only 22 years old and he never remarried.

In the old Thompson cemetery on top of College Hill in St. Albans, there is an impressive obelisk, nearly twenty feet high, erected in 1834 in memory of Dr. John Thompson's wife.

Of course Dr. McGinnis became very popular with the young folks. When he boarded at Uncle Joe Capehart's we girls, that is four or five cousins, saw him often and became very intimate. Bettie Wilson (now Chilton), Thenie Capehart, Priss Wilson and Bettie Thomas were grown and had quit school. One day he told us he was going to give all the children a "candy pulling." That was what we called making molasses taffy and pulling it white. It was a very popular amusement and he wanted us to come and superintend the making on the appointed evening.

We girls all got on our horses and took one of the little ones on behind us. As cold and muddy as it was we were all there in due time. Aunt Martha told us that the doctor was gone to Rose Hill, the residence of Jesse Hudson. He was invited to a very select party of full grown ladies, and Aunt Martha supposed he had for-

The obelisk erected in 1834 in memory of Dr. John Thompson's wife. AC

gotten all about the candy pulling. Of course the children were disappointed and we were mortified to think that he should forget us as we considered ourselves as big as anyone. We played and ran and laughed as girls will do until we got tired.

Bettie Wilson proposed sending for Dr. McGinnis and we joined in the idea in a minute. We did not dare let Aunt and Uncle Capehart know or to send any of his servants. So we decided to send two of the boys that came to the candy pulling. We were delighted at the idea. We even blacked the boys faces to look like the Negro boys and made them take our horses for it was three miles. We told them to call for Dr. McGinnis and say that Miss Bettie Wilson had been thrown from her horse and had broken her arm. After they left we laughed, played and cut up and even told Uncle Joe what we had done.

When we saw how dry and serious he looked we began to think what we had really done and began to settle down. Most of the children and girls hid and declared they would not see him if he came. We soon heard the boys coming back and we ran to meet them. We wanted to hear if they had carried out the joke fully and hoped that they had not. But they said he was coming and had only stopped at his office to get his

splints and bandages. They said he was at the table when they got there and came out to see them, but did not recognize them. He went back and bid the company good evening as he would not finish his supper.

Being a young doctor he was pleased to be sent for. After a while he came and when he rode up to the house everything was quiet and no one met him. He then began to suspicion that something was wrong. Uncle Joe Capehart was walking up and down the porch when Dr. McGinnis came up to him and asked where Miss Bettie Wilson was. Uncle Joe said she was in the house and said there was nothing the matter with her. Dr. McGinnis blazed out, and wanted to know if Uncle Joe had anything to do with sending for him. They were both very high tempered men and we girls were by the window listening and feared there would be a fight. They all pushed me forward saying he thought more of me and I should tell him. I walked out very slowly and said "Dr. I hope you will forgive us, I will take all the blame."

I think it was in '44 that Aunt Tildy had a paralytic stroke. She had started to go see her daughter Jane who belonged to Uncle Felix. She always went once a year on horseback. Uncle Frank had a horse of his own. She had started and got some distance on her way when she was taken and fell off of her horse in the road. Someone found her and brought her home and she got all right. Then about six months later I was down at their cabin sitting and talking to her and Uncle Frank about their chickens. He had dug a cellar under his cabin for his hens to lay in so they would not get mixed with ours. It was so warm and nice that they would lay all during the winter when we could not get any eggs. Aunt Tildy who was a great smoker got up and went to the fire to light her pipe and over she fell on the hearth.

Uncle Frank picked her up and laid her on the bed. I ran to call Nellie and Jane to come there was something wrong with Aunt Tildy. She never spoke but laid and snored as if she were asleep. I went for Father, he knew immediately what was the matter, she was dead in the morning.

I know how bad I felt and remember that there was to be a party at Frank Thompson's that night. When they sent the paper to me I wrote "declined." I thought it would be disrespectful to go and her a corpse.

It was the custom at that time to send a list of names of all invited and you would write "accept" or "decline" after your name. I think it a nice way as then it was known how many they might expect. Another advantage was you could tell if anyone was going to be there that you did not wish to meet.

Father advised me to go as Mary Lasley was depending on me to take her in our buggy. So I went and that was the first place I ever danced as all of us were young and still going to school. After that I loved to dance and never missed an opportunity. The Lasley girls and myself would practice every evening, taking our little chairs as partners. Father never allowed dancing in his house as he was a member of the Baptist church, but he never forbid me from dancing. He said he did not see any harm in it for young people who were not members of a church, unless they made harm by going to pay balls.

Not many years after this three French men came to the neighborhood and two opened a dancing school. They had it in one room of the Turner's house at the mouth of Coal River. The old house is still standing, as I pass it I often think of the merry times we used to have there. I attended regular as the Frenchmen boarded with us. They had a large school, it was in '46 or '47, I have forgotten which, that

The Elms. PHK

the three Frenchmen came to Coal. One taught French, one dancing, and one was an artist and took Daguerroetypes, the first that was ever seen here. The one who taught the language was named Feasare and the dancing master was Laurestes. I took French lessons and could read and write my exercises very well, and he complimented me on them. He had quite a large class and taught two sessions. His family lived in Charleston.

The French teachers were sons of John Francis Faure, who was born in the town of LePrey, France in 1794. He served as an officer under Napoleon and came to America in 1816. After the prescribed number of years residence, he became a citizen of the United States in 1828. He was an architect and in 1822 he designed and built "The Elms" for his bride, Eliza Dryden, the widow of Samuel Dryden. She was the daughter of Col. Alexander Quarrier.

After the death of his wife in 1837, "The Elms" was sold to Judge James H. Brown, one of West Virginia's most eminent jurists. Since then the stately mansion and its grounds have been identified with the Brown family and remained like a down-town Charleston park until only a few years ago.

The John P. Turner House, built about 1832. Restored in 1990 by William and Carol Graley. SAH

When Quarrier and Alderson Streets were extended, they intersected on the exact site of "The Elms," thus sweeping away another landmark in the name of progress.

Father would not have let me go to dancing school if it had been any place but at Col. Turner's. They were the best people, his wife was old Col. P. Thompson's daughter. They had six children and several Negroes and were generally hard up and glad to rent their room. There was no one who came but the nicest people. Two of Col. Turner's children were grown at that time, Charley and Sallie. Sallie was a beauty, one of the sweetest girls and greatest favorites in the place.

Col. John P. and Helena (Thompson) Turner had two sons who died on the same day while serving in the Civil War. Charles Philip and Theodore Garnett Turner both died on December 30, 1861, of typhoid fever at Giles Court House, Virginia. They had volunteered in the ranks of the Kanawha Riflemen, commanded by Captain George S. Patton (grandfather of General George S. Patton, III). —The Vandalia Journal, April 1973, pub. by the Upper Vandalia Historical Society.

About this time there was a Mrs. Joplin and her husband who came from Richmond, Virginia, to old Mr. Swindler's. They were some relation to them. Mrs. Joplin went all through the neighborhood to get up a large school, mainly for girls, except she took small boys. She had a good English education and professed to teach everything taught in high schools plus fine embroidering and drawing. She could embroider beautifully and she taught cross stitch. She also worked on canvas and perforated bristol board. It was all new to us and we girls were wild to learn. There was not a nice girl in the neighborhood that did not go to her school. She taught in the big log church which I suppose would seat 200 easily. After she taught the first session, everyone was so pleased that the next term she had a great many young ladies from a distance.

She boarded at our house and also several of the young ladies. There was a Miss Madaline Thompson from Teays Valley, also her cousin, Amazetta Thompson. A Miss Smith and Bettie Hansford boarded with us also. There were at least 15 or 20 grown girls going to school to her.

At the same time there was a boys school taught by Mr. Nash, the Episcopal minister. He was highly educated and was from Connecticut. At that time he was living in the Episcopal parsonage where the Potters had lived when I took music lessons there. It was a nice large frame house and had a smaller house in the yard that he used for a school room. Most of his scholars were grown or nearly so. He had boarders from Charleston, Wheeling, Buffalo and Point Pleasant. Of course these two schools made the place lively and cheerful as the girls and boys often met and had nice times.

I think the two schools were a stimulant to each other. Most of the scholars studied well and tried to outdo each other at their examinations. Mrs. Joplin was a good teacher and had experience in how to carry on a school and to make it popular. The girls all seemed to like her. At Easter time the scholars determined to have a holiday and go fishing over at the Falls of Coal. We were going to take our dinners and spend the day.

We all had begged and pleaded with Mrs. Joplin to give us a holiday but she would not give her consent. Therefore, we determined to take it, so the scholars all came to the school house very early and prepared to turn her out. That is we all got inside, locked the door, fastened down all the windows and would not let her in until she gave her consent. She pretended to be very angry at first and tried to break the door open. She even got a man to help her pry the windows open. I always thought that she was as pleased as we were to have a holiday. After she gave her consent and we opened the door, she was in the best of humor and as full of fun as we were.

Some of the boys from Mr. Nash's school got an inkling of what was going on and came ready to join the fishing party. We had plenty of help to fix our fishing poles and to get bait while we prepared our luncheon baskets. It was over a mile to the falls but we soon walked it and what a glorious day we spent. Of course there was not many fish caught as the girls and boys were too fond of talking and laughing to fish much. We got home in time for supper, tired and hungry and ready for a good night's sleep. Oh, those were happy days.

Mrs. Joplin also gave us a May festival, it was on a grand scale, everybody came for twenty miles around. Cousin Lizzie Thomas was the queen. She made a beautiful queen, she was so dignified. She had six maids of honor all dressed with white flowers in their hair. Each one said a piece appropriate to the occasion. The whole affair was the same as I have described at Miss Sarah Kiger's school when I was a little child, except it was later in the month. It was on the 17th of May, Cousin Lizzie's birthday. We put it off that we might have plenty of flowers and we certainly had. We had a May pole with a wreath of flowers twenty feet long. It was made of all the large showy flowers such as snow balls, peonies and lilies. They were tied on a rope that could be wound around without breaking. There was an elegant dinner set in a long arbor back of the church. The queen and her maids of honor which were Mary Lasley, Bettie Wilson, Bettie Hansford, Madeline Thompson, Mat Hudson and myself, Mollie Hansford, all marched from the throne to the table. All the girls were strewing flowers in front of us. We also had military music, drum and fife played by two little dwarfs named Dudding, one of them is still living.

Uncle Joe Dudding was one of the little people Mollie referred to in the military band. He was born in 1830 on a farm where Lake Ridenhour in Nitro is now located. He was the son of William and Nancy (Persinger) Dudding.

Uncle Joe was said to have been a happy little person who was a favorite with the children and grown-ups alike. He spent most of his time visiting around from one farm to another in his neighborhood. He would play with the children and do odd jobs for awhile and then move on to the next home on his circuit. He would return home and would be content there until he began to miss his many friends again.

In his later years he grew a long beard and it is said he was a living image of one of Snow White's seven dwarfs. He lived to be 74 years old, dying in 1904. —Kanawha Valley Leader, Nitro, West Virginia, January 29, 1960.

At the close of our school that session we had a public examination. That is what is known now as a commencement. We had a grand time then, each of the larger girls had to stand up and read their own compositions aloud. I only remember that mine was on music.

All the girls that had taken embroidery lessons had a nice piece to show and each one wore

Joseph Dudding, 1830–1904. AC

a velvet apron worked with flowers in cross stitch. Six of us had a wreath of roses worked on fine white canvas with our names in the center. These were done in beautiful moss work. I had mine framed and hung up to show. Several of the girls had other nice pieces. I had one on a square of black cloth with a white cat lying on a red cushion. It was all done in cross stitch and it was a foot and a half square. I had it made to cover an ottoman.

It was difficult to get anything of that kind then but I had seen several and was determined to have one. There was a cabinet maker living near us so I went to see him and described exactly how I wanted it made. I took him the cloth and told him to make it that size out of walnut or cherry. He made as nice a one as I ever saw

and everybody admired it. I also got him to make me two music stands like some I saw in Charleston. I cut the patterns out of paper for him and he copied them exactly. He said afterwards that I was the cause of him getting as much new work as he could do. No one before seemed to know that he could do anything but the most common work. I had a little money of my own that Father would let me have for anything like that. I had these things made in 1848 so it has been 50 years ago and I still have the ottoman and one of the stands.

When I married and left home I took nothing with me but my clothes because I had to go so far away. Not even things that belonged to my mother that I should have kept. I did not even take my scrap books that I had been making for years. I always thought I would get them when I would come home on a visit, but when I came it was never convenient for me to take them. Another thing I disliked taking them from the girls, they had so few nice things and I did not need them. So for that reason I never got any of my father's or mother's things. Not even the things of my own that I had made and paid for. I did not care, however, except to have some little things for my children to keep.

Cousin Bettie Hansford only stayed one session at Mrs. Joplin's school. Nor did Madaline and Amazetta Thompson, they were cousins and were from Teays Valley. Madaline was very delicate and only lived a few years after she left school. She was very pretty, had dark brown hair and eyes and very fair skin with regular features. Amazetta was not as pretty but she was very bright and funny. She afterwards married a Mr. Herndon and one of her sons is now living in Charleston. He has some public office and his mother lives with him.

Amazetta Thompson was born in Hurricane in 1833. Her parents were Robert Napoleon Bonaparte and Julia Anne (Morris) Thompson. Her father was born in Augusta County in 1812 and her mother was born in Cabell County in 1812. Their house was burned during the Civil War by Federal forces of the 34th Ohio Regiment. —Hardesty's History of Putnam County.

When Cousin Bettie Hansford was living with us Brad Noyes used to come to see her. He was not very handsome but he was a good musician and also an artist. He used to paint portraits. John Ruby used to come with him some times, for fun I suppose. He afterwards married May Noyes, a sister to Annie Hansford. Cousin Bettie married James Middleton who was a son of old Henry O. Middleton, a great land owner and speculator. She married several years after I did.

MRS. JOPLIN'S SCHOOL was broken up by her having cancer. It was an awful one on her breast. When it first commenced coming it was like a little ball under the skin. She would show it to me and ask me to feel it as it would seem to move. It grew very fast and was soon as large as a hen egg. She then became uneasy about it and someone told her to go to see an old man in the valley by the name of Mynes. They said he could cure it and tell her if it was a cancer, as he had cured many. She got me to go with her and we rode horseback. I remember when we got there I did not like the old man's looks. He took Mrs. Joplin into another room and examined her and said he could cure her. He said she must have faith and come back three times. She was very much encouraged for a time. It soon got worse, however, and she went to Charleston to Dr. Parker, a Yankee doctor form New York, and was considered to be no one. Nothing did any good, poor woman, she went on teaching with her breast as large as a man's head and as purple as a damson. When school was out she went to Gallipolis to a regular cancer doctor who burned it off with caustic. It must have been awful.

When she came back I was at Paint Creek on a visit. I always went up once a year, Bettie Hansford and I were such great friends since we were little kids. After she boarded with us to go to school we became greater friends than ever and we kept up a brisk correspondence. Even though every letter was 6¼ cents, we considered that cheap as they had been 10 cents. I do not remember of us ever having a cross word or a falling out as most school girl friends do. Although I went to visit grandmother Hansford and made that my headquarters, Bettie and I were always together. Oh, those were happy days and we certainly enjoyed our blessings fully.

I remember when Bettie went home from our house. Her brother Felix, or Cousin "Dy" as we called him because his father was also named Felix, came on horseback to get her. "Cousin Dy" and myself were about the same age, a little older than Bettie and he was our constant companion and playmate.

Father had sold Uncle Felix a horse that Dy was to ride home and Bettie was to ride his. As I was going home with them I rode my own horse, a pretty little gray named Mike. Father had got him from a traveler who swopped him because his back was sore and he was obliged to continue and needed another horse. Father had a large fine bay that was almost blind that the man took for Mike and was glad to get him. No one could ride Mike for months and when they did try he would jump and squat almost to the ground because his back was so tender. Mike was only three years old when we got him and he became a faithful and good horse both for saddle and carriage.

The horse that Father had sold to Uncle Felix was a large dark blue gray. We called him "Blueskin" because he looked so blue.

As I was saying, we three, Bettie, Dy and myself rode horseback the thirty miles from Coalsmouth to Paint Creek in one day, as we usually did. It was very warm, dry and dusty and we did not realize how tired we and the poor horses were. When we came in sight of Uncle Felix's we saw several ladies on the front porch with Uncle and Aunt Sallie. Dy said let's ride up in style. And child like, we put the whip to our horses and rode up to the gate in full gallop with dust flying. I remember how Uncle Felix looked, he was a very firm and dignified man. He always looked very severe and as a child, I always stood in awe of him as did his children. He did not say a word but helped us off. As the Negroes came to take the horses, he took Dy off and gave him a good lesson in private, we never forgot it.

We spent our time at Paint Creek walking or riding and climbing the mountains. We waded in the creek and often pushed up and down on a wide plank with poles.

Once we went with Uncle Milton Hansford up Paint Creek about five or six miles where he was getting out lumber. He had several men and a Negro woman to cook. We went on horseback and crossed the creek fifteen times. There was only a narrow bridle path, the mountains coming down to the creek on both sides. The mountains were covered with laurel in bloom. It was perfectly beautiful and so wild we never passed but one house on our way. When we got to camp there were two shanties, one to sleep in and one to cook and eat in. We ran about and gathered wild flowers and trimmed the room with bunches of laurel and pine until we were called to dinner. How we did enjoy it, had tin cups for coffee and tin plates. We had a big "dogger" of corn bread and fried fish. It was splendid, old Aunt Pat really knew how to fry fish. Uncle Milton had brought some little extras from home on purpose for us, such as butter and dried fruit stewed. He was so full of fun and made it so pleasant for young folks as he was young himself.

Uncle Milton had lost his first wife and did not keep house but boarded at Grandmother's with his little son and daughter. Several years after this he married again, a woman that no one in the family considered his equal in any way. Grandmother particularly was so offended that she would not permit him to bring her home. So he built himself a house up the creek that I understood was about where the log camp "Shanty" was. He lived here the rest of his life and raised a large family.

Uncle Milton was Grandmother's youngest child and her favorite. Poor thing, she was so proud of her family and it seemed that she could never get over his marriage with this woman. My father said, however, that he went to see them during the war and found her a plain, kind-hearted woman that made him a good wife. She knew how to do all kinds of work and seemed devoted to him.

The first wife of Uncle Milton Hansford was such a perfect lady and of the best family being a great niece of George Washington. The two children by this marriage had very fine advantages. The son however was killed in the Confederate Army at Gettysburg. Their daughter married a respectable man but poor, Mr. Chapman that came here soon after the war from south-west Virginia. He was an engineer. As I was married and gone when Uncle Milton married the second time, I never saw his wife.

The first wife of Milton Hansford was Mary Parks, daughter of Andrew and Harriet (Washington) Parks. Her mother was a daughter of Samuel Washington, a brother of General Washington, who raised her after her father's death.

After the death of Washington in 1799, a life interest in Mount Vernon passed to his widow. In her will she left the majority of the household effects to her grandchildren and favorite nephews and nieces. This caused the original furnishings of the mansion to become scattered. Mary (Parks) Hansford eventually came into possession of a two-part dining table with serpentine ends and reeded legs. This special treasure is still in the Charleston area. —Pioneers and Their Homes on Upper Kanawha—Dayton; Hardesty's History of Kanawha County.

I must go back to when I returned home and Mrs. Joplin was there. When I got home I found her there, she insisted on me looking at her breast or at least where it was taken off. I was very tired from my long ride and when I looked I fainted and for some reason it seemed to offend her. She did not stay with us much longer as she moved up to Mr. Swindler's for awhile and then went to Gallipolis where she taught school. I heard however that in a few years the cancer came back lower down and killed her.

Poor woman, there was a great deal of talk about her and I look back now and I know that she was not always what she should have been. I must say though that she had so much to contend with her husband. He was no account in the world except to play the fiddle and drink. He was not unkind to her as is generally considered unkind but he did not support her, but he did not support himself either. He did not seem to care for her or sympathize with her in her affliction. Although she sometimes acted badly she was always good and kind to me and taught me a great many things.

I was now grown although so small that I did not look over fifteen. I was invited to all the parties and I always dressed as well or better than most of the girls in my circle. I had good taste so I was told and loved to sew and made my own clothes. I would always have something original, I would never copy after others. Many of the girls would come to me to fix them when we were invited to a large party.

It was about this time that William Henry Thompson who was an officer in the U. S. Navy was married to a lady in Louisville, Kentucky.

He brought his bride here to see his relations. They gave them a reception at Ben Thompson's and I was there. It was the grandest affair of the kind I had ever attended. It would take too much time to describe it. They were in our neighborhood several weeks but never returned. Some years later he was brought back all the way from California in his lead-lined coffin to be buried in the family grave yard. Now all his relations are living in California, and his wife is buried in Louisville. It only shows how foolish it is to carry the dead from place to place.

William Henry Thompson was born at Coalsmouth in 1820, the son of Philip R. and Sarah (Slaughter) Thompson. He served six years in the U. S. Navy as a midshipman and died aboard the U. S. Sloope Warren off the California coast, March 15, 1851, on the eve of his promotion to a Lieutenant.

His body was sent back to Coalsmouth and he is buried in the Thompson cemetery on College Hill. —Hardesty's History of Kanawha Co.

AC

It was about this time that Uncle Sam Wilson and Aunt Thenie got a teacher for their girls and took in some other girls. I attended mostly to take drawing lessons and French. This lady's name was Miss Mary Gilpin. She was an old maid from Philadelphia and was educated in England. She was a refined lady and highly educated but was very eccentric, all northern people are so different from southerners. We girls had lots of fun doing all kinds of things to shock her and to play tricks on her. She had a great horror of fleas and would walk a mile out of her way to keep from meeting dogs that she thought might get them on her. We got some of the little children to catch all the fleas they could off of a cat. We put them in a little box and took them to school with us. We passed it around and pretended to try and hide it until she made us bring it to her. When she pulled the top off, out jumped all the fleas on her. She quickly dismissed school while she went to her room to change clothes. She had a high temper and very little patience but she did teach me a great deal about drawing.

It was while I was going to school to Miss Gilpin when Cousin Pattie Hansford was married to Mr. Sam Smith. She had written to me that she wanted me to be one of her brides maids. Miss Gilpin thought it was awful for Father to let me go to the wedding and that he should not let me be an attendant, since I was only a school girl.

I was delighted to go of course and I made myself a dress of white tarlton which was very fine and sheer. It was tucked to the knees with a very full plain skirt. All the attendants were dressed alike except all of the other girls had white Swiss muslin, trimmed with Swiss edging. Everyone thought my dress the prettiest although not as serviceable as theirs. Mine could not be washed but it lasted me many years, as, for parties, I would press it out and alter it occasionally.

I had a nice time at the wedding and did not return to Coalsmouth and school for some time. Soon after Miss Gilpin left and went to old Virginia to teach at Staunton. I later heard of her during the War Between the States when she was arrested for being a Yankee spy. She was arrested and taken to Richmond and I never heard of her afterwards.

After she left I used to take drawing lessons from a Miss Sarah Farechild, another Yankee teacher. She was teaching at Mr. Alford

Ravenswood, located on MacQueen Boulevard in St. Albans, traces its history to the 1830s when a frame dwelling was constructed on the property. The present brick structure was built in 1833 by Francis Thompson. The house had several owners until Judge J.B.C. Drew purchased it in 1897. Trading on the name Ravenswood, he fabricated a story that Edgar Allen Poe wrote his famous poem, "The Raven" in the home. Extensive remodeling was undertaken in 1914. PHC

Thornton's and I liked her very much. She was a maiden lady and I learned more from her about drawing than any other teacher I ever took from.

Mr. Thornton had a large family, all daughters but one. Sallie was the oldest and she was so sweet and affectionate and I liked here so much. She was younger than I but unlike me she was large for her age and looked as old. She was so romantic and full of sentiment. She was far from being a beauty but she was so bright and striking in her appearance. She had large soft brown eyes, a turned up nose and I thought a beautiful mouth. Her father was wealthy and she had everything that they could get her. They had one of the finest and sweetest pianos I ever heard or saw. It cost them a thousand dollars and was brought from Germany.

They lived at what is called "Ravenswood," the place Cousin Frazier Hansford afterwards bought. It is a beautiful place but so lonely. It had five acres in yard and five in forest and trees. The last time I ever saw Sallie was the morning I was married and passed there leaving for Old Virginia. She was in the yard near the road with several others to bid me farewell. Poor dear, she turned out badly, her story was a romantic one that I cannot tell here.

"Ravenswood" was built by Philip R. Thompson, Jr. and was deeded to Alfred Thornton in 1852, after he had lived in the house for several years.

In 1859, James Frazier Hansford acquired the estate and he and his wife Annie (Noyes) Hansford lived there until they died. Family tradition holds that since some of the payments on the mortgage were made with Confederate money, a judgment was brought against the es-

During the course of time, a dozen or more owners have made changes to the house and grounds. One of the most noticeable alterations was when the original buff brick was coated with stucco.

It was while I was going to school here that one of the young men in Mr. Nash's school ran off and tried to hire out and work on a farm. He went several places but of course they did not want him. His name was Wilcox and his father was considered wealthy. He lived above Malden on the south side of the Kanawha and owned a great many slaves.

This boy who was about eighteen did not approve of slavery so Mr. Nash sent him home as he had to do. He did not stay there long however but induced two of his father's Negroes to run off promising to go with them. He then went to Charleston, forged his father's name and got two hundred dollars out of the bank. He also persuaded another Negro belonging to lawyer Ben Smith to go with them. (Ben Smith married a cousin of mine.) He got a large skiff and he sat in the back pretending to read a newspaper while his servants were rowing the boat. They started out in full view of everyone along the river and no one suspected that he was stealing his father's Negroes. When they got within a few miles of Point Pleasant they knew they would be running a great risk in passing.

They landed on the north side of the river and took to the road. They were soon captured, at least Wilcox and one of the men. The others got away but young Wilcox was brought to our house to be tried before Father. We were then living at Coal Bridge where my sister now lives. It was beautiful weather and Father held the court, or trial, in the front yard under the large beech tree that is still standing. He was sent on to Charleston to jail. His father bailed him out, paid all things and sent him off to Kentucky.

The Wilcox boy was Lewis, son of Luke and Pinkston (Kenner) Wilcox, who came to Kanawha from New York about 1818. His father settled near present Marmet and soon was engaged in the salt business, acquiring two furnaces near his home.

Lewis was established in Kentucky by his father, where he lived out a long and useful life. Another brother, John I. Wilcox who also attended Mr. Nash's school, became a doctor and lived in the old home place at Marmet. —History of Charleston and Kanawha Co., W. S. Laidley; W. Va. Historical Magazine "Coalsmouth," 1903.

I wish I had more time and space to write about the different boys and girls that attended the two schools. There were so many romantic incidents connected with them.

There was a young Mexican that was brought to Coalsmouth by a Dr. Wood who picked him up in Mexico during the war (Mexican War 1846). He brought him home with him to educate and try to make something of him. He was very bright and soon learned to speak English well. He was very much in love with me and annoyed me greatly with his attentions. At last, however, he started back to Mexico and wrote me a letter from Independence, Missouri. He said there was a family living there by the name of Hansford.

I always thought it was some of Uncle Herman Hansford's family. He was Grandfather's oldest son and he moved to Missouri long before I was born. None of his family ever came back to Kanawha that I knew of. Years later one old Negro that he had taken from here as a little boy came back. When he returned, everything was so changed that he did not know the place and all of his playmates were grown and married and had forgotten him. Poor old fellow, he seemed heart broken, he said he had always remembered his old home as being almost paradise and all the folks, both white and black, as being the best on earth. The blacks that were his playmates would have nothing to do with him and treated him as an imposter. Two of his former white masters were as kind as they could be but he soon tired of trying to find sympathy and went back to Missouri.

5

Soul Searching

OH, THERE ARE MANY such cases when a few years change everything and you are soon forgotten. You look back and remember, and time and distance lends enchantment to our memories. Then if we can return we find all things changed and not as we expected. We must make our own homes, be they ever so humble, and learn to accept our place and surroundings even though they may be very different from what we had in our youth. They will eventually become as dear to us, as we love our own families and realize that home is where'er the heart is.

Life is too short to waste in regrets. We must enjoy the present and make the most of every passing moment. Jesus says, "work now for the night is coming, in which no man can work." I often look back now and think of the precious moments and hours I have wasted in my life and would give anything now if I could recall them.

I try to fill every moment of my time now by doing something for others. I would not be writing this sketch of my life now if I did not think it might be of some benefit to my grandchildren when I am gone.

There are so many times that I am not able to do anything but write. It is strange but it does not hurt my eyes to write as it does to read, yet my eyes are good for one of my age. I am in my seventy-first year—this day April 22, 1899.

I must say I was never one to complain or find fault with my surroundings and I was never discontent or envious of others. One might think I am bragging on myself but I am not because it seems to be natural with me. I have often been sorry for girls who were always unhappy because they did not have everything their neighbors had. They could not enjoy the present for looking forward and wishing for something else they imagined better.

Although my childhood was not the brightest and I was never petted and loved as most children, I was content. I can truly say that from 1843 up to 1853 I was as happy and enjoyed life as much as if my father had been wealthy and I had of been his only child. He was always so kind and did everything in his power for me. St. Albans (as it is called now) was a pleasant social place and there were so many nice families living there.

John Lewis was one of the wealthiest men who lived in Coalsmouth. He had three sons and an only daughter by his first wife. His daughter was several years older than I was but I can remember when she got married while I was going to school to Mrs. Joplin. What a grand occasion it was, she had a Catholic Bishop from Cincinnati to marry her. She had been educated at the Catholic Institute at Bardstown, Kentucky, and while there she met the man she married, a Mr. Kenna who was a young educated Irish gentleman. Her father gave her a farm at Droddy Falls on Coal River. Mr. Kenna was a lawyer and of course knew very little about farming and she knew less.

She had been a petted, spoiled child who had ruled everyone around her. It was said she was hard on her slaves and that she had no mercy when angry but was kind and indulgent when not. She and her husband never lived happily. They would part every once in awhile and she would go home and stay a month or so. After a time they would become reconciled and would live together again. This went on until her father sold out and moved to Florida where he died.

We had a black man named Wesley that had married Mrs. Lewis' house maid. Father tried to buy Wesley's wife that they might not be parted. Father never would part any of his colored families without they requested it. Wesley wanted to be sold to Mr. Lewis after he found Father could not buy his wife for him but Mr. Lewis could not buy him. Neither would Mrs. Lewis hire her maid out or let her stay away. Father let Wesley go and stay with his wife as much as he could.

Mr. Lewis' daughter, Mrs. Kenna, remained up Coal River on the farm after her father moved. A sad thing it was then, she could not go home and stay awhile as she had always done. They lived so unhappily that at last they sued for a divorce. It was not an easy matter to get a divorce at that time in Virginia. You scarcely ever heard of one and a divorced person was looked on as disgraced. When the suit was to be tried in Charleston, she found that her husband was about to bring very disgraceful evidence against her. She then sent word to her brothers, asking them to help prevent it, as her father was then dead.

All three of her brothers came to Charleston and went to the hotel where Mr. Kenna was staying. When the "gong" sounded for dinner and all the guests started for the dining room, the three brothers fired at him at once. They walked out of the hotel and crossed the river in a waiting boat where they had a fine two-horse buggy waiting to take them away. There were no railroads or telegraphs then so they left the country and indeed no one tried to stop them. They never returned but it is said that during the war one of them came back with the Army.

The full account of the death of Edward Kenna was carried in the Star of the Kanawha Valley, June 15, 1856, copy on file at the West Virginia Department of Archives and History.

A later edition dated November 4, 1856, gives the report of the Circuit Court of Kanawha Valley "Bringing indictments against Andrew B. Lewis, John W. Lewis and James V. Lewis (brothers). for the killing of Edward Kenna, last June, at the Kanawha House in Charleston."

Mr. Kenna was dead and he left a son and two daughters. The Catholic priest took his son, as he had requested, and educated him. He became a lawyer and rose to one of the first statesmen of West Virginia. He was elected to Congress and was a United States Senator when he

John Edward Kenna, 1848–1893

John Kenna was born at Valcoulon in Coalsmouth. He attended school in Wheeling, eventually becoming a lawyer in Kanawha County. In 1876 he was sent to Congress becoming one of West Virginia's most distinguished statesman. He was so honored when West Virginia dedicated a statue of him in Statuary Hall in the National Capitol. AC

died. He died young, everyone liked John Kenna.

His mother went to Missouri and there married again, a man by the name of Richard Ashby, a very nice gentleman. They came back to Charleston after the war and she had one son by Ashby. The son, Walter Ashby, is a lawyer and is now living in Charleston. Her daughters married nice men and their descendants are living in Charleston also.

Walter Ashby had a son Joseph Ashby who became the first postmaster at Nitro, in 1918.

I mention this incident to show how much it depends on ourselves as to how things are in the world. She had everything to make her happy but she was never contented. She gave away to her passions until she brought sorrow and disgrace on herself and family.

Of all the rich and fine families that lived at Coalsmouth at that time there is not one left. What few descendants that are still here are now poor. Our family stands now about the same as it did then, neither rich or poor but good livers. We were highly respected, truly moral and religious. We never made any exertions to be at the head, or to make a great show to live in grand style beyond our means.

The Lewises and Thompsons lived as near like the English nobility as they could. John Lewis was ahead of all, he had a regular shepherd, hired a Scotchman with his shepherd dogs. He also had a park with deer and elk. His Negro quarters were a nice little village, he required them to plant vines around their cabins and they were always white-washed. Every spring his own residence was as nice and beautiful as any English villa. The grounds surrounding were full of beautiful rare trees and shrubs of every kind. The kitchen yard and garden were divided from the others by a beautiful hedge.

I was at a large party there once long after his daughter was married and he had married his second wife. I shall never forget what a grand affair it was. The double parlors were thrown into one with heavy yellow damask portiers looped back between. The floors were waxed until you could see yourself in them and they were dangerous to awkward persons. One young man, Phil Thompson, fell full length on the floor as he entered the room. They could not get him to come back in again that night, he was young and bashful.

I danced every set, I was dressed in white mull with a white satin sash and white kid gloves with lace at the tops, short sleeves and low neck with lace. It was in the fall of the year and I wore a wreath of white wax berries on my head and a bunch with green leaves at my belt. They had a splendid supper and we danced so late that all the girls stayed all night, about twenty of us. As usual, Mary and Sallie Lasley had come with me and my cousin, Charley Capehart, drove us in our carriage.

The next morning when we started home, there were five or six carriages all started out at once. Mr. Thornton's large two-horse carriage, like hacks are now, was in front, with a Negro driver of course. Charley was very wild and wanted to be ahead of everything, so he must cut out our one horse and pass all the other carriages. When we came to a sudden turn in the road, the trace broke and over went the carriage. The horse ran on breaking it, of course, and leaving us girls lying on the side of the road. My face and arms were scratched and cut considerably and I was covered with blood. I looked more hurt than I really was. Sallie hurt her back so she could not walk for several days and Mary escaped entirely. The other carriages came along and took us up. I remember Sallie Thornton said she wished it had been her because I looked so romantic lying there on the road-side covered with blood.

In 1820, John Lewis, a grandson of General Andrew Lewis bought up one thousand acres just below Coalsmouth from the lower end of the Thomas Teays tract of land extending back to the headwaters of Tacketts Creek and to the waters of Brown's Creek. Next to the hill John Lewis, known as "Coal River John Lewis," built a large brick mansion which he called "Valcoulon," named after John Savery de Valcoulon, first owner of the land, and to this home he brought his bride, Caroline, a daughter of Andrew Donally, a prominent man in Kanawha Valley. Valcoulon was of Colonial design, the main part was three stories with a large ell to the west of the house. The rooms were very large with very high ceilings. The woodwork was painted white and each room had a very high mantle with wide open fire places. Two wide halls, upper and lower, ran the length of the house into which many rooms opened. A spiral stairway led to the third floor. This third floor was turned into an emergency hospital during the Battle of Scary in 1861. Note: one of the mantles from this home is now in the home of Mrs. Fred Staunton in Charleston.

The deer and elk park, located across the old stage road (Route 17, now Route 35) has been referred to in varied descriptions of this home. It is told that a colored man's sole duty was keeping dogs from molesting the deer and peafowl, considered a mark of affluence. The lake or fish pond was near where the railroad now goes through. The first race track in Kanawha Valley was constructed on this land.

Valcoulon, antebellum mansion below Coalsmouth, built in 1820 by John Lewis, was the headquarters of Capt. George S. Patton before The Battle of Scary.

John Lewis established a large three-story mill, about one and one-half miles below his home on the river, together with a general store around where several other people lived. Ira Lasley was clerk and bookkeeper; Michael Persinger, Herman Gentry and many others made up a large percent of the citizens of old Coalsmouth's village. The mill proved a failure on account of the location, and it was moved to Coal River, where it received the Coal River and Mud River patronage. John Lewis came to Coalsmouth a wealthy man, he was owner of many slaves but through bad management and extravagance he lost most of his wealth.

Mr. William Tompkins of Cedar Grove bought Valcoulon and it was here that Camp Tompkins was located at the beginning of the Civil War. The home was next owned by Colonel C. B. Swann who gave the name to the river landing known as Swann's Landing.

The house fell into ruins and about 1916, the site was purchased by the Roesler and Hasslacher Chemical Co. The house was razed and the plant and surrounding houses for the employees were built. The section was called Chemical City. The chemical plant is now gone and a drive-in theater is on the site of the house.

Uncle John Capehart's family was considered rich. Charley was living at Point Pleasant in business with his uncle. Thenie was then going to school, Aunt Betsy visited and entertained with the best, had her own carriage and Negro driver. She was always very kind to me and used to take me with her to the associations, as I had no one to go with as Father could never leave the tavern. Aunt Thenie and Aunt Martha never visited except with each other, nor let the girls go to any of the dancing parties.

It was some time in fifty-one that Uncle Joe Capehart moved to Missouri and Cousin James Teays moved back from Guyandotte during the forties. He opened a store on the road just below the old log church. They were Methodists and still hung to the old church after the split. Their house became the home for the Northern Methodist preachers. All the other Methodists in this place belonged to the Southern M. E. Church.

THERE WAS A PREACHER by the name of Adams. I heard him preach a sermon that deeply convicted me. I do not now remember the text but only part of the sermon. He said there were a great many persons belonging to no church but were as true Christians as those that were in the church. He compared them to fine stalks of corn outside the fence. They grew luxurious and many looked better than those in the field. One day, however, the cattle came by and ate them down to the ground. If they had been inside the fence they would not have been disturbed. Thus, it was with those outside the church, they might grow fine for a time, but there were so many temptations to lead them astray. The evil ones would say: "You do not belong to any church, why not join the dance, or the card parties, such things would draw your mind from all things serious and your convictions would soon pass away." Therefore, it was best for those under conviction to join the church on probation and then strive for conviction by prayer and leading a good life.

I thought that the more I could mortify my pride the better it would be as I sincerely wanted to be a Christian. I knew by experience that I could not keep away from dancing and card parties in my own strength. I thought the laws of the church would keep me all right, not knowing that it was not abstaining from these things alone that made a Christian. If I had been truly converted I would not have wished to partake in any such amusements but would have been thinking of doing God's work and loving Jesus with all my heart and trying to make others love Him.

I was trying to make myself a Christian by joining the church and mortifying myself as much as possible. So I joined the Northern Methodist church which was at that time looked on as almost a disgrace by all of the best people. I joined but was not taken in full membership as I could not decide the question of baptism. My father was a Baptist and thought immersion was right, if not absolutely necessary.

I read and talked but never became reconciled. Thus, it went on for years until after I was married and went to Virginia to live. My husband was a Methodist and his father was a Methodist preacher. I was thrown altogether in a Methodist society and had one of the best religious libraries. I went to a camp meeting and I was again deeply convicted. The Lord did not give me over to hardness of heart but He had mercy on me. I again joined the church in the fall of 1854 and thought at the time I was converted. For a long time I thought I was all right and imagined I was ready and willing to die.

THEN AGAIN I FELT as if I did not care what became of me and was perfectly reckless. I did not care what I did or what I said or read and I would not look into the Bible. During the war I had such hatred in my heart for the Yankees, it seemed years and years after the war that I could not forgive them. I had so many trials that instead of doing me good it seemed to harden my heart. I know now that I was not truly converted nor did I have the love of Jesus in my heart. I had too much pride and relied on myself too much.

Then all at once my pride and self-reliance were taken from me and I saw myself as I was. Then I turned to Jesus with my whole heart and soul feeling He was my only hope. As soon as I gave myself to Him, He gave me such deep sweet peace and love. I felt as if I loved everybody in the world and wanted everyone to feel as I did.

Many would not believe me when I say I never get angry as I used to. I feel hurt at unkindness and ingratitude from those I love, but I only feel sorry for them, that they cannot see as I do. Knowing that if it is the Lord's will they will see it some day as I do. I feel so thankful all the time for my many blessings and I never worry over worldly matters. I feel it is all in the Lord's hands and all we have to do is do unto others as we would have them do unto us.

If we give ourselves to Jesus and love Him, all things will work together for our good. Life is short, let us make use of the present to glorify Him and we will be happy and that is what everyone is striving for in this life. No one but those who have truly renounced the world and given themselves wholly and fully to Jesus can realize that sweet comfort and peace to be enjoyed in this life. My prayers all the time are that my children may find this peace.

I have always abstained from preaching to my children fearing to disgust them. I felt that I had not set the example as a Christian that I should have. I had given away to my temper and not controlling my tongue by saying things that set them a bad example.

6

Friends, Neighbors, and Relatives

I MUST GO BACK as I was telling of the different families at Coalsmouth at that time. There were four Thompson families, each of them with a fine farm and a number of Negroes. They all had families except Dr. John Thompson, his mother lived with him. She kept the children of Robert Thompson who was a Congressman, his wife being dead. He had two daughters and several sons and he lived in Charleston before his wife's death. Miss Mary Rogers, Aunt Betsy Capehart's sister, was governess for them. Miss Mary was very delicate and after her sister married she quit teaching and lived with them.

Col. Philip R. Thompson settled at Coalsmouth in 1816. Here he erected the family homestead and called it "Muckamore." All his life he was an ardent supporter of the Democratic party. A noteworthy event in the history of the area took place October 5, 1832, when Andrew Jackson, then President of the United States, paid Col. Thompson a visit in his home at Coalsmouth while on his way back to the capitol.

Col. Thompson was twice married, his first wife was a Miss Davenport; by her he had three children; Philip R., Jr.; Eleanor, who married Dr. W. G. Thornton; and Eliza, who married Ricker Fry of Richmond.

His second wife was Sarah, a daughter of Col. Robert Slaughter of Culpepper County. They had the following seven children; Robert A., Francis, John, Benjamin, William H., Helena, and Sarah.

Helena married John Turner of Coalsmouth; William H. died in the Navy, Robert A. was twice married; first to Mary Slaughter and his second wife was Elizabeth, a sister of General Jubal Early. His daughter, Mary, married General Ord of the U. S. Army.

Col. Thompson laid out Coalsmouth into lots and renamed it Philipi and he was also co-builder of the first bridge across Coal River.

Most of the Thompson families eventually moved to California before the Civil War. Col. Philip R. Thompson, his wife and several of his children are buried in the Thompson cemetery on top of College Hill in St. Albans.

The Thompsons of Coalsmouth were one of the most illustrious and influential early families that settled in the Kanawha Valley.

The father, Philip Rootes Thompson, and his son, Robert A. Thompson, are both listed in "Who Was Who in America" —Historical Vol. 1607–1896.

Philip R. Thompson, *Congressman, lawyer, born near Fredricksburg, Va., Mar. 16, 1766; grad.. from College of William and Mary, studied law. Admitted to bar. Member of Va. House of Delegates 1793–1797; member of U. S. House of Representatives. Democrat from Va. in 7th and 9th Congress 1801–1807. Died in Kanawha County, Va. (now W. Va.) July 17, 1837, buried at Coalsmouth (now St. Albans) W. Va.*

Robert A. Thompson, *Congressman, lawyer, born Culpepper Co., Va., Feb. 14, 1805. Attended Univ. of Virginia, studied law, admitted to the bar in 1826. Began law practice in Charleston, Va. (now W. Va.), member of Va. Senate 1839–46. Democratic presidential elector 1844; member of U. S. House of Delegates from Va. 30th Congress, 1847–49. Delegate to Democratic National Convention at Baltimore in 1832. Moved to San Francisco, Calif. in 1853. Appointed on committee to settle land claims in Calif. 1853. Aptd. reporter for Calif. Supreme Court 1870; Justice of Court of San Francisco 1870–1876. Died San Francisco, Aug. 31, 1876.*

The first time I was ever in Cincinnati I went with Miss Mary Rogers. I was going to school but Father let me go. Her brother, Major Rogers, was boarding with us at the time and he was going for his summer goods. He was also going to take his sister and she insisted on me going with her. I had very little clothes to go with except one nice worsted dress I had made myself. The only wrap I had was a coarse plaid yarn shawl. I wanted Father to get me something but he said since he could not afford to do that I could take the black silk dress of my stepmother's. He said it would not be of any use to the children and that it had been laid away so long it had cut in the folds. I took it and cut me out a cape very much like those worn now. Father got me some pink silk called "sansinetts" to line it with. It made a pretty cape and I was very proud of it as I had made it all myself.

When I told Bettie Wilson (now Chilton) her mother, Aunt Thenie, was very much shocked at my taking the dress. She even gave me a lecture, but I could see that they were jealous because Miss Mary who lived next door to them had asked me instead of Bettie. Of course, I could not help that.

Soon after we got on the steam boat we got acquainted with a Miss Sallie McConihay and her brother Ira who were also going to Cincinnati. Charley Capehart was also making the trip so we formed quite a party. I had met the McConihays once before and liked them. Although they were plain country people they were kind-hearted and had plenty of money. Sallie was delighted to have a lady friend with her so we put up at the same hotel and took the same room. Charley Capehart and her brother did the same. They attended to us and went out in the city with us while Major Rogers was getting his goods. Oh, we had a glorious time as neither of us had ever been in a large city before. We had never seen a museum or attended a theatre in our lives. I remember one play was "Lucrezia Borgia" where she poisons all of her guests and they die at the table.

Ira and Sallie McConihay's parents were John and Mary McConihay who were early settlers in the Kanawha Valley. Their home was at the mouth of Field's Creek, about fifteen miles form Charleston. John McConihay owned a large tract of land, valuable for its coal, timber, and farming purposes. He was an active, energetic business man and he was the head of a large and respectable family. —History of Charleston and Kanawha County; W. S. Laidley.

Soon after this trip I was invited by Mary Morris, a daughter of John Morris of Teays Valley, to be her bride's maid, as she was to be married to Ira McConihay. John Morris was considered to be one of the richest men in Cabell County at that time. Ira McConihay was the young man that was with us in Cincinnati and he lived above Malden. His father was also wealthy in coal property.

Ira came down in a buggy bringing his attendants with him. Each one in a buggy to take the bride's maids with them. The gentleman I was to stand with was named Hurt. He was from Old Virginia and at that time was renting and running a salt furnace at the Licks. It was in the spring but I do not remember the month. It was quite cool and we had to wear wraps. The roads were very muddy and we had to drive very slow, but that was the only way we could go except on the stage.

We had a grand time, we were young and full of life, and mud and cold made no impression on me at least. I remember how foolishly I was dressed to travel in a buggy 20 miles, but I could only carry one dress and I had to wear the other one. I carried the white one I was to stand up in and I wore my other nice dress which was a purple brocaded silk. It was one of the richest looking dresses I ever saw but I was obliged to wear it even if it did look out of place. I know they all thought it vanity in me. I did not care and I was one that never told my own affairs.

It was one of the real old-fashioned weddings of that time. In slavery time it was possible to entertain 50 guests with their horses. As to the supper, it was beyond description. The table was covered with the richest of everything served in the most elegant silver, china and glass that was not common at that time.

Mary looked pretty, she was a plain country girl as good and industrious as she could be. The next morning after the wedding, the bride and groom and all the attendants left for his father's at Malden, there to have a grand infare, as it was called. We got there at night and the fine dinner was the next day. I was from home a week.

I never saw Ira and Mary again for many years, then only for a short time. They had several children and I once worked a dress for the oldest one. Her son, Dr. McConihay now lives in Charleston. Ira died and Mary married again, a Mr. Sibral of Monroe County. I never saw her again until I was a widow and she was also, for the second time, such is life.

Mary (Morris) McConihay was the daughter of John Morris who was born in Culpepper County, Virginia in 1794. In 1819 he married Mary Kinard. He lived east of Milton in Cabell County and was an extensive stock raiser. He was frequently elected to the Legislature and was known as a man of wealth.

When the Civil War broke out, John Morris took his slaves and went east. in his absence, his house was burned inflicting a great loss on his family. Before he could return home he died in 1862. Still another tragedy brought about by the war was suffered by the family. Captain Joseph W. Morris, who was Mary McConihay's brother, was killed at Frederick, Maryland, while serving in the Confederate Army.

Mary and Ira McConihay were the parents of John M. McConihay who was born on the farm in 1853. in 1876 he graduated from the Kentucky School of Medicine. He began his practice in Leon, Mason County, and then moved to Buffalo in Putnam County. In 1880 he transferred his practice to Charleston where for over thirty years he was one of the prominent medical men of the city. —History of West Virginia, Old and New; —History of Charleston and Kanawha County, W. S. Laidley.

7

Social Life in the 1850's

B UT I MUST RETURN to my girlhood, it was during these years from 1846 to 1853 that I had numerous beaus, or I should say offers of marriage. I do not know why, as many were much prettier and equally as smart and intelligent, and many much more so.

There were two things I knew I was ahead in. One was good taste and the other I was industrious. I never was called lazy. I made all of my own clothes, besides those of the children and I was always very neat in my dress, be it ever so poor. Yet, now since I have lived to know more of the world and had more experiences, I can see one reason I had more offers. I had property in my own right, land and Negroes left by my mother.

I will repeat over the names of the gentlemen as they are all, as far as I know, dead and gone, so there will be nothing dishonorable in me doing so. Some of my grandchildren may meet some of theirs and remember their ancestors were friends.

First was E. Lasley from Louisa, Virginia; Rob McGinnis from Cabell County; Mr. Daubin from Mason County; Will Parrish from Kentucky; Dr. McGinnis, Cabell County; Andy Anderson, Loudon County, Virginia; and last Dr. Walls of Winchester, Virginia, whom I married.

I had plenty of other beaus that made love to me and sent me presents and took me to entertainments. They were the most pleasant companions in every way. I tried to prevent them from asking me to marry. I knew that I would refuse and then they would cease their attentions. I loved attention but did not wish to marry at that time. I loved no one and it was nice to have someone bring you flowers and books and to take nice boat rides with, and all that. Although young ladies that were respectable at that time never received expensive presents from gentlemen, one gentleman made me a cross out of a mussel shell. It was tipped with gold and there was a gold ring to hang it by. He also made me a ring of the same, they resembled pearl with a pink shade, they were beautiful. Another gentleman made me a ring of cannel coal with a silver heart on top. There was also a charm to hang on my watch chain. It was a small book tipped with silver in the corners. They were all very pretty. Cannel coal can be polished as jet. I prized these presents because they had been made for me. I had several handsome gold rings offered me but never accepted but one and that was an engagement ring.

I was never engaged to but one gentleman before Dr. Walls and Father was very much opposed to that. I broke it off and returned his ring. Dr. Walls brought me a handsome breast pin or broach with his likeness in it. It cost fifteen dollars but I would not take it and told him to keep it until we were married. When he came on to be married he brought me a handsome gold watch and chain but I never wore it until after we were married.

Will Parrish, the young man from Kentucky, was here on a visit to his Uncle Louis Bowling. James Bowling, his cousin, was a very bashful young man and would not take him around to see the girls. He got Mr. Redmond Rust whose farm adjoined Bowling's to come with them up to Coalsmouth and introduced them to some of the girls. He brought them to see me and Cousin Bettie Wilson (Chilton) and Lizzie Thomas. They stayed a week visiting from, house to house, as was customary at that time and we girls enjoyed it. James Bowling never talked any and we made fun of him. Poor fellow, he was a kind-hearted, good young man and his father was rich. The

This house was built by Lewis Bowling around 1848. At the start of the war Bowling had 125 slaves, whom he attempted to march back to Old Virginia. Most of them, however, managed to escape on the way. Both armies occupied the house, using it at different times as hospital and headquarters. It is still standing near Nitro and has been well preserved. RAC

girls all liked his cousin best even though he was a plain farmer. After he went home to Kentucky he wrote me asking me to marry him, I never saw him afterwards.

James S. Bowling was the son of Lewis L. Bowling who was born in Amherst County, Virginia in 1794. He brought his family to the Kanawha Valley about 1838 and settled below present Nitro. Soon after he built an impressive house that is still standing near Rock Branch in Putnam County. It was said that Lewis Bowling owned 125 slaves and if a guest was invited for dinner he would be expected to sit down at a large table with the Bowling family and all of their house servants.

James Bowling married Martha Ann Tyree of Fayette County in 1859. Her father was of the family that operated the well-known Tyree Tavern at Ansted.

In 1861 when the Union Army began advancing up the Kanawha Valley, Lewis Bowling headed east, on foot, with all of his people. He got as far as Gauley Bridge before he was forced to abandon his plan. Returning home without his servants, he had no one to work his fields. A few months later when the great flood of 1861 ravaged the valley, he suffered a financial loss from which he never fully recovered. —Hardesty's History of Putnam County; Recollections of Albert Sidney Morgan.

After Aunt Betsy Capehart was married to Mr. Wyatt and left the Capehart home, William, the oldest son, was living in Point Pleasant. He came up and insisted on Father taking the farm and the home place over. He also wanted Father to take his sister Thenie to board with us and to have him appointed her guardian. I was perfectly delighted with the idea. This was in 1850 and we had been living at the bridge in the tavern house for ten years. I was tired of it and wanted a more retired life and I did all I could to get Father to go. So we moved and how happy and delighted I was with everything. It was a large brick house with seven nice rooms, two long porches at the back, one below, and one above. There was a veranda in front and a beautiful yard full of ornamental trees and arbors covered with roses and honey suckle. It looked out on the Kanawha River with the public road running in front of the gate. It had one of the prettiest old fashioned gardens with every kind of flower you could mention. There were all kinds of small fruit trees and also a large apple and peach orchard. We had as many peaches as we had apples, they never failed except when all the other fruit did.

Oh, that was a beautiful pleasant home. Thenie came to live with us and we roomed together. There were two beds in the room and Vic and Cint were with us. Vic slept with Thenie and Cint with me. Tildia, the colored girl, attended to the room, her sister Nellie tended to the milk, butter and the dining room. Jane, my woman, cooked. At that time she had five boys, we would often bring her baby upstairs and mind it when she was busy and the other children were all out at play. It was a good house for the colored people as well as the white. Old Uncle Frank lived in one house with his children and Jane in another. Jane was such a faithful good woman.

I had a riding horse of my own and Thenie had one also. Her horse was a beautiful little bay named Natala. Mine was a jet black that I called Jet. Father had my mother's saddle done over for me and had it covered with blue cloth; it also had a bright red girth. He paid twenty dollars to have the work done. I bought myself a light tan colored bridle. With the light bridle and blue saddle on my black horse, it looked beautiful. We would ride every day to the post office, every evening that we could, it was just a mile from where we lived. There was always a Negro boy ready to get our horses when we wanted them.

Although I missed my friends Mary and Sallie Lasley after we moved, yet we had plenty of company. Aunt Thenie lived in sight on one side and Cousin Mary Ann Teays on the other. We also had Bettie and Puss and Lizzie Thomas, we were either at their homes or they were at ours. Every day we would have little parties. When any one of us had other company we would invite each other over. We used to have all-day quiltings and invited the boys in the evening for plays or to sing. Thenie brought her piano with her and she was a good performer. I knew very little about music as I had given it up on account of not having a piano. Yet, I could play by ear a great many tunes and we sang together.

There is one friend of mine I never mentioned that used to visit us often. It was Mary Hudson, she was the daughter of Samuel Hudson and lived two miles above St. Albans. She had six brothers, all older than she was and she was a great pet at home. They were very well off and lived in comfort and plenty on their farm. They gave nice parties and I have passed some of the most pleasant days of my life visiting there. Her mother was such a warm-hearted, plain and practical woman. We girls always did as we pleased there and she was always in good humor and had a nice dinner or supper ready for us. The girls in our neighborhood would make up a party of four or five and walk up there. On long summer days we would be up and on the road by sun-up. We would get there in the cool of the morning and stay until nearly sun-down in the evening before starting home.

After the war, Mary married a man from southwest Virginia named Hufford, and they had one son. Her brother Willis was a devoted admirer of mine.

There were two other Hudson families living in that neighborhood. Her father was Sam Hudson and his brother Jesse Hudson lived almost in sight and had a house full of girls and only two sons.

One of his daughters married Samuel Washington, a near relation of General George Washington. He had his cane, a sword, and some other things that he presented to Congress, thinking I suppose, he would get something for them as he was poor, but they never gave him anything.

Captain Samuel Washington was the son of General George Washington's youngest brother Charles. Samuel received the sword that General Washington carried in the field which was referred to as the "Battle Sword." Samuel also eventually inherited from his father, Benjamin Franklin's gold-headed cane. George had given it to his brother Charles after he had received it through the terms of Dr. Franklin's will.

Captain Samuel Washington also inherited two tracts of Washington's land in the Kanawha

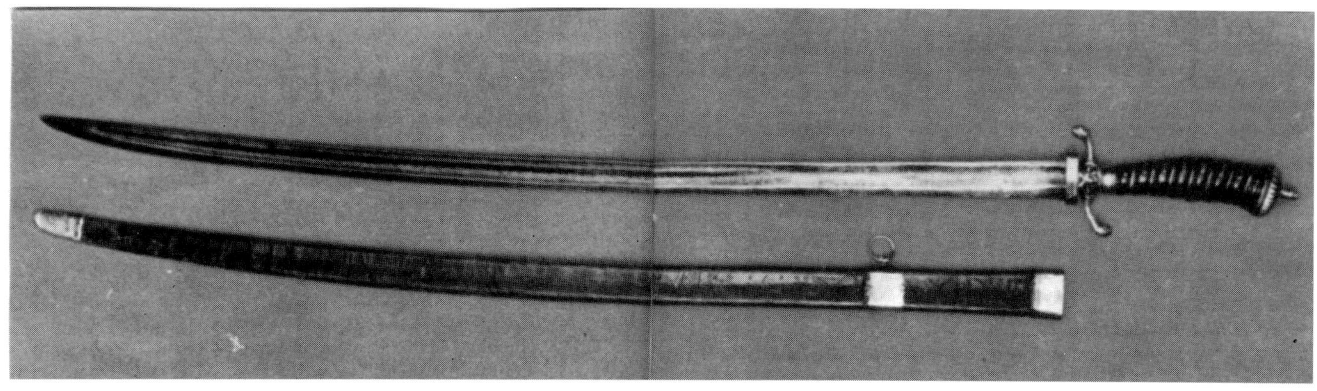

George Washington's battle sword, presented to Congress of the United States, February 8, 1843, by Samuel T. Washington of Coalsmouth. AC

Valley. One containing 2,233 acres was located below the mouth of Poca River. The other parcel consisted of 1,330 acres which ran along the river from the lower end of present Dunbar, extending below the site of the Union Carbide Chemical Plant.

Because of his land interests in the valley, Samuel Washington moved his family from Culpepper County in 1816 and located on his upper tract. About the same time, Philip Roote Thompson, who had been a distinguished neighbor in Culpepper County had also moved his family to Coalsmouth, now St. Albans. Eventually the Washingtons moved across the river to Coalsmouth where there was already a neighborhood community consisting of the Hudsons, Thompsons, and Thorntons.

Samuel and Dorthea (Thornton) Washington had four sons, Samuel T., Jr.; Augustine C.; George F.; and Francis A. Samuel T. Washington, Jr. married Wilhemina Hudson in 1828 and they established their home at Coalsmouth. Later Captain Samuel Washington removed to what is now Putnam County and died at Frazier's Bottom in 1831. Many of his descendants are now scattered throughout the valley, one in particular was a great-grandson, Cline W. Grant of Nitro.

Two other daughters married brothers. Another married Dr. R. Thornton. One of the brothers, Robert, married a Miss Salisbury and the other one went to Missouri. Mrs. Robert had a sister Mag as we called her, she was very wild with black eyes and hair. She married Dr. Ed Bailey, a half-brother to Sam Smith who married Cousin Pattie Hansford. Dr. Bailey was the son of Judge Bailey of Lewisburg, and they moved to Georgia some time after they were married. I attended the wedding. They were living in the house now owned by Judge Worth. She had a grand wedding but it was a very cold night. I remember all the girls were dressed in white with short sleeves and low-neck dresses, except myself. I wore purple silk, high neck, and long sleeves. Judge Bailey came up to me and remarked that I was the most sensibly-dressed girl there.

After we moved to the Capehart place on the river, there was a family moved into the John Lewis farm. Col. Roswell Grant, an uncle of U. S. Grant, had married his second wife who was a very nice lady, a Miss Jane Kemper. Mr. Grant had three daughters and a son. They were one of our nearest neighbors and we became great friends that lasted through life. Tom Grant died in the Confederate Army. One of the daughters married a Mr. Baldwin and had two children. They are now living in St. Albans.

Roswell M. Grant was the father of the family that Mollie referred to. Mr. Grant had the distinction of being an uncle of General U. S. Grant, yet during the Civil War, his son Thomas C. Grant was killed in the Confederate Army. These close connections with both sides led to a continual harassment from whichever of the opposing forces happened to be in the area at the time.

R. M. Grant wrote a letter from Mayslick,

Kentucky, September 7, 1874; "After follow-ing my trade for twenty-eight years, I quit tan-ning, bought me a farm of seven hundred acres on the Great Kanawha River, nine miles below Charleston. . . . During the late war I was an-noyed by both armies, I rented the farm out and came here in 1862."

The seven-hundred-acre farm referred to was part of the original Valcoulon estate at Coalsmouth sold by John Lewis to William Tompkins. Tompkins was a prosperous salt maker who in 1844 built his home at the mouth of Kellys Creek which he called "Cedar Grove." At the beginning of the Civil War his remaining Coal River property was used for a Confeder-ate training area and was known as "Camp Tompkins." Tompkins' wife was Rachel Grant who was a sister of Roswell Grant and an aunt of U. S. Grant.

Roswell M. Grant was 86 years old when he died in 1886 and he is buried in the family plot in the old Tompkins cemetery on College

Roswell M. Grant's tombstone. AC

Hill in St. Albans. —St. Albans Historical Soci-ety Journal, Fall 1974; History of Charleston and Kanawha County by W. S. Laidley.

Thenie and myself went to Point Pleasant to visit the families of her Uncle James Capehart and Dr. Shaw. She boarded with the Shaws a long while when she went to school there. We stayed mostly at Dr. Shaws as they lived in town and her uncle lived in the country, although he had a large store in town and would go in every morning. His son-in-law, Will Smith, attended to it as he lived near by and was a partner. Will Smith's wife was Olivia Capehart and she died on her bridal tour as they were returning home. He was a widower at the time we were there and he paid us a great deal of attention. He gave me a handsome book "Philopens" while I was there. Dr. Shaw had five daughters, his oldest Maria, was about my age, she was a good sweet girl but not pretty. She had been on a visit to our house some time before.

We had a pleasant visit there, we had plenty of beaus and were invited to several nice places where we got acquainted with the Hendersons, McCauslands, Roseburys, Smiths, McClintics, and Stribblings.

We went back out in the country and stayed a week at the Capeharts. He had married a Miss Couch who was his second wife. When we were there she had two children and I offered to help her with her sewing and embroidered a dress for her baby son. Thenie did not like her much and thought it foolish of me to do it, as she had a regular seamstress. But I did not look at it that way, it was a pleasure and amusement to me in that lonely country place.

They lived in a sweet, beautiful place and the house was considered in those days to be el-egantly furnished. It was kept in perfect order but of course they had plenty of servants to do it. I shall always remember the dining room, how sweet and bright it looked every morning. Two large windows looking east with a pretty bird cage hanging between them, containing two beautiful ring doves. I do love nice bright din-ing rooms.

We returned to Dr. Shaws and he took great pleasure in showing me his beautiful flower gar-den. He was very fond of flowers and so was I.

Maria was his only daughter that was con-

REGULAR GALLIPOLIS AND KANAWHA
RIVER PACKET

THE FINE STEAMER

JONAS POWELL,

W. L. MADDY, Captain,

Leaves Gallipolis every Mon.. Wednes. & Friday morning.
Leaves Charleston every Tues., Thurs. & Saturday morn.

The finest accommodations will be found on the Powell,
she being the largest boat in the trade.
no9-tf   J. B. GATES, Clerk.

RAC

New Gallipolis and Kanawha
River Packet.

The new, fast, and elegant Packet,

VICTOR No. 3,

Capt. WM. L. MADDY,

Having been purchased for this trade, will

Leave Gallipolis every Monday, Wednesday
  and Friday mornings,   at 6 o'clock.
Leaves Charleston every Tuesday, Thurs-
  day and Saturday mornings,   at 9 o'clock,

The Victor No. 3 will afford every accommodation to
both passengers and shippers.
n23tf   W. L. RUFFNER, Clerk.

sidered grown at that time. Mary later married a Mr. Cargle who was a lawyer and lived in Winfield. Becky married Dr. Carpenter and lived in Poca. Maria married a steamboat captain named Maddy but I never met him as I married first and left the valley.

I have said so much of my visits and parties that one would think I was always in a round of pleasure, but this was not so, those visits and parties were scattered over years and years. There was a great deal of sickness and displeasures in the meantime.

The cholera was brought here by steam boats that came up the river. There were many deaths on the boats and in Charleston. I do not remember but one death at Coal and that was a colored man belonging to S. Thornton. However, there were a great many persons who imagined they had it. Everyone quit eating vegetables but Father said he did not think that was right to abstain altogether and eat nothing but bread and meat. He thought we should be very temperate in all our eating. I was always a very small eater but continued to eat fruit and vegetables as usual. Mary Lasley was taken very sick with diarrhea and thought she had the cholera but the doctor told her she was only frightened. He asked if I would go and stay with her, make light of it and see that she took her medicine and to cheer her up and she would soon be well. I did so and it turned out as he said.

As the summer passed the people commenced to get the dysentery from living on bread and meat alone. There were whole families down at once. Uncle Wilson was very ill with it and came very near dying. Mr. Lasley's family were all more or less sick. I would go every night and sit up with the sick to give them their medicine. I would go just at dark after supper and leave next morning at daylight when the fog would be heavy. I would go regularly to bed and sleep until I was called to dinner, in this way I remained well.

The epidemics of the valley began first between the years of 1813-14. It was a very grave and fatal form of fever with such ominous symptoms that physicians were at a loss as to what to call the disease. The second was an epidemic of influenza in 1832, called the cold plague, of which many died before diagnosis could be established.

*The following year, 1833, was the first visitation of **Asiatic cholera** to the valley. It first broke out at the Kanawha Salines, brought in by the river men from the cities along the Ohio. It again appeared in 1848–49, from which the valley suffered throughout its entire extent. It reappeared three years later, in 1851–52, except this time it was only prevalent in various localities. The final scourge of this dreaded disease returned in 1866 but with a death rate of only about twenty percent of those afflicted. —History of the Great Kanawha Valley, Vol. II, page 258.*

Bettie Wilson, Lizzie Thompson and sometimes Thenie would go with me to help with the sick and we went two together generally. We sat up and attended one poor woman that died the next morning soon after we left. Her husband and family came in to take charge of her, she seemed better. She was the wife of Dick Hughes; he afterwards married Lizzie Robinson and had a large family.

We did not go to nurse those of our own class of friends, but mostly the poor class who did not have Negroes to do anything for them. The Negroes would feel insulted if we had asked them to go, they called them "poor white trash." We did not mind going, however, and they never thought of visiting us afterwards. We would generally take a lunch in a basket to eat during the night and sometimes they would propose to make us a cup of coffee. Often we would send them a basket of food that we knew they did not have. Yet, as a general thing, most lived well and had plenty as at that time there was none very poor in Coalsmouth.

At that time there were two distinct classes, nearly the same as there was in England. Money made no difference, it was the family. Very few of the second class had any education as there was no force schools. They never mixed any more than oil and water. Yet all these people I would nurse when sick and would go and see them when they were in trouble. They all seemed to like me and would come to me to help them cut out patterns and to borrow new ones. It never seemed to enter their minds to come as visitors or invite me to come to see them as they do now.

The slaves always thought themselves above these people. The greatest slur they could give each other was to call someone "poor white trash," or a "free Negro." It was not so bad here as it was down in Old Virginia as we were so near the free states and there were not nearly as many Negroes here. the whites in the lower class were better off in many ways then, than they are now. Yet our house servants were more refined and better mannered.

Nelly, our house girl, a tall fine looking mulatto, would say to me when the girls would come for me to help them with their sewing; "Miss Mollie, I don't see how you can stand dat poe white trash hangin' around and sittin' about in your room." The Negroes always called the higher class "quality" and would have nothing to do with anyone they considered lower.

Most of the sickness I remember was between 1849 and 1853. I was always very delicate but was never sick in bed except when I had the measles. One fall while we lived at the bridge I had the ague with chills and fever but it only lasted about a week. Father always doctored us chil-

dren himself. He did not believe in giving much medicine. I always bragged that I never had a doctor to see me until Dr. Walls came courting.

Father always taught me to take care of myself. The other girls would go boat riding bareheaded and would wear thin shoes getting their feet wet and making them sick the next day. I would always have something on my head and wear overshoes. The girls would laugh at me and call me grandmother but I did not care. Thenie was a picture of health and plump with rosey cheeks. She would often say "if I had to be as careful as you I would stay at home." Now she has been dead over thirty years and I am still living.

Of course we are all in the hands of the Lord. Yet He has given us our bodies and He expects us to care for them and follow the laws of nature as near as we can. Some people think it is so nice to be thought of as a very healthy person. They will try to prove it by doing all kinds of imprudent things knowing that they will pay for it later. They are afraid the public will think they are delicate or sickly so they suffer to please others. It would be better to be thought of as weak and delicate than to sicken and die in early life, or be helpless in your old age.

T HERE ARE VERY FEW of my school mates now living. I am still delicate but not helpless and my mind is as good as ever. I can still sew, embroider, draw and write. Besides, I clean up my own room, sweep and dust and mind my own fire. I try to set an example for those around me. If I am at all well I never get up after eight, but as a general thing I get up by six or seven. I try to keep myself always busy and try to always be cheerful.

I never worry or fret now, I used to worry myself if things did not go as I thought they should. I look back now and see how foolish I was. I was really sinful, for the Heavenly Father controls all things. We are expected to obey God as near as we can and do all things the best we can in His sight. He will see that the righteous are not forsaken and whatever comes is sent by Him for our good. I see and feel this more each day I live.

We must all have trouble and have enemies, but our greatest enemy is old Satan. He makes us resist the Holy Spirit that would come in our hearts and give us peace and happiness. If we would but give ourselves up to Him instead of trying to make ourselves better by our own efforts. We always fail, we make rules and resolutions that we will do better and will not give up to our passions. We soon break them however and find out how weak we are in our own strength. Then old Satan makes us think it is impossible to be a Christian and so it is, unless we give ourselves up fully to Jesus and learn you can do nothing by yourself.

I NEVER WAS ONE TO LOOK on the dark side of life; if there was any brightness I generally found it. I do not take any credit for this as it was my natural disposition. No two are alike, some are naturally gloomy and see everything at its worst. Yet I think that it can be overcome by always resisting it. I know myself there are many times I find myself looking on the dark side because I am not well. When my body is out of order I am wrong physically and that affects me mentally if I give up to it. I find I can resist it if I truly try and pray as I should for the good Lord to help me. He can make me see things differently and receive them as coming from Him. If we think someone has treated us badly or has done us a great wrong, we feel as if we have no true friends and everything looks dark. That is the time to try our faith and look on the bright side and ask help from our Heavenly Father. We know He is always ready and willing to help us and comfort us, if we will only give ourselves wholely to Him.

We should forget what we consider slights and unkindnesses, we are prone to find fault and we often take to ourselves what is not intended for us. Even if it is, we should look over it and forgive. I often hear persons say, "never mind, I will pay you back," or "oh, so they will not do so and so for me then I will not do such and such for them."

I know by myself there are many things I would do for others if I could think of them at the right time. No two persons are alike, some are very thoughtful of little things, while others never think, until it is too late. Some persons, if they like you and look on you as a friend, will ask you to do favors for them that they would not ask others and never think they are imposing on you. Then you will expect them to do the same for you under all circumstances. I have known persons who imagined that they were badly treated and slighted because someone did not return every little favor with interest. For my part, I always try to return all favors for I always feel under obligation until I do unless it is a particular friend.

If we noticed every little thing and worried and talked about it, we would always be miserable and everything would look dark to us. We cannot see as others see or make them see as we do. Therefore, take things easy and ignore the bad, and remember the good. Above all, never throw up things that have passed and would be forgotten if left alone. Some people are so cruel that they will never let an old sore heal but are always opening "for fear it will be forgotten." Oh, how cruel and un-Christian-like—but forget myself. I am trying to write some incidents of my life. I must stop moralizing.

After we moved on the Capehart farm where we were so pleasantly situated, I had more time to visit. At that time Aunt Kitty Sutherland was living in Maysville, Kentucky, and often wrote and insisted on me coming to visit her. I finally persuaded Father to let me go for a few weeks and I went on a regular packet running between Charleston and Cincinnati named the "Blue Ridge." Father put me under the care of Capt. Tom Hope whom he knew very well. I had a pleasant trip and I was on the boat two days and nights. On Sunday morning before we got to Maysville I was sitting out on the guards looking down on the water when I saw a man floating by. His face was turned up to the sun and his hair was floating out on the water. (Men wore long hair at that time.) I screamed that there was a dead man but the Captain seemed to take it very cooly. He called to some men on the shore and told them to send out a skiff and get him. I suppose they did as we were soon out of sight.

In the year 1846, Warth and English built a large packet boat at Cincinnati, designed to run between that city and Charleston which they christened the "Blue Ridge."

Capt. James A. Payne of Red House Shoals sent an agent to Cincinnati and when the "Blue Ridge" was ready to come out he purchased her.

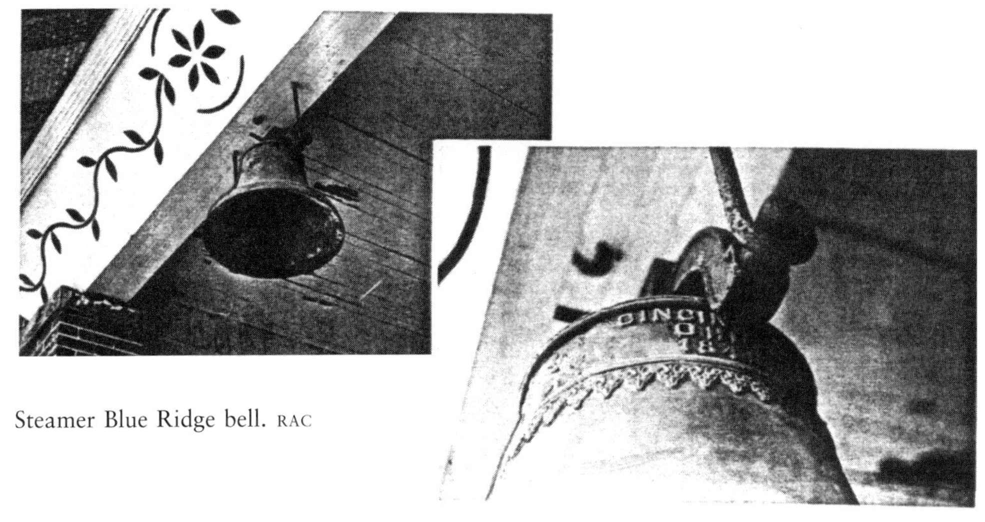

Steamer Blue Ridge bell. RAC

He put her in the trade for which she had been built, with Capt. William Summers first in command.

She continued to make regular trips for two years. It was then that she exploded her boilers four miles below Gallipolis. Many persons now residing along the river remember the sad disaster by which fourteen persons lost their lives. Among the killed were Joseph Miller of Point Pleasant, John Carr of Buffalo, William Whittaker of Charleston, Francis Samms of Gallipolis, Albert Chapman, P. Carpenter and a Mrs. Mayse.

The original bell from the ill-fated "Blue Ridge" now hangs over the main entrance inside the Putnam County Court House. —Hardesty's History of Putnam County.

I found Aunt Kitty living in Abberdeen, a town in Ohio just opposite Maysville. Her mother-in-law and brother-in-law, John Sutherland, lived in Maysville where he was a tobacconist. He had a large store and they lived nicely as I was there several times. Everything seemed so strange to me in Abberdeen. I never had stayed any time before in a free state where the ladies did their own work. It looked strange to see Aunt Kitty doing her own cooking and washing, however, she got along nicely with it, she was so systematic, she had everything at regular hours. She had two little girls, Alice and Bettie, and she had them washing the dishes and putting them up. They could do many little things that were a great help. They had a nice play house in a large box where they kept all of their play things. They were not allowed to play all over the house and tear up things generally as most children do.

I had a pleasant time and I was invited out to supper while there. It was the first place I had ever seen the lady of the home get up from the table and wait on the guests while her husband was keeping the flies off with a feather brush. I could scarcely eat I felt so out of place since I had always been accustomed to servants waiting on the table. The lady of the house would have thought it a disgrace to leave her seat to attend the table, or even to give orders that anyone could hear. Eventually I got to like it and they had very nice eating as Aunt Kitty had learned to be a good cook. While I was there the first volume of Uncle Tom's Cabin came out and Dr. Sutherland bought it. I remember that I was so foolish and prejudiced that I would not read it since I had heard so much about it.

I returned from Aunt Kitty's on the same boat I went down on. It was not long after this that Thenie's brother William died in Point Pleasant. He was brought back up to Coal to be buried in the old family burying ground. By this time it had been moved from the old home place at the mouth of Coal to the hill opposite the old log church that grandmother Teays had given. It was a beautiful situation on the hill. My father, Uncle John Capehart and all the son-in-laws of Grandmother picked out the site and decided on the hill. They had all the dead in the old graveyard taken up and moved there. Grandfather and Grandmother Teays had large stone boxes over them, they are not very pretty but they are durable. They have now been there seventy years and are as good as when moved. After they had decided on the place and before any of the dead were moved, my step-mother, Maria Morris Hansford, died and was the first one buried there. Now it has become the public cemetery and has been added to. It is such a beautiful place that everyone wanted to bury their friends there until it became impossible to refuse. Now they require all to buy their lots and it is known as the Teays Cemetery. It is truly a beautiful place and will improve as the years pass as everyone will improve their own lot.

At one time I thought I must be buried there and we talked of buying a lot as Mr. Rust was so pleased with the place. About a year after we were there and talked about it he died and was buried in the old family graveyard here. So now, I will be buried by him as it makes but little difference where we are buried. A few years change everything, families are scattered, burying grounds pass into other hands until our descendants may scarcely know where we are buried. It is not like it is in England and other countries where the land is entailed and always kept in the family.

The history of the Teays Cemetery has been well documented back to 1878 when the Teays Cemetery Citizens Association was organized and incorporated. Down through the years this organization has remained strong and faithful.

Before 1878 Teays Cemetery was used mostly by the family and their relatives and friends. No records were kept except for the tabulations on the individual stones.

The inscription over the grave of Stephen Teays indicated he died March 20, 1823. His son William's death, however, was noted as occurring in 1818. It was always taken for granted that these were the oldest graves in the cemetery.

The disclosure by Mollie that her step-mother, Elizabeth Teays Hansford, who died in 1842 was actually the first person buried there has thrown new light on the cemetery's beginning. The fact that the original Teays graveyard was at the mouth of Coal River and was moved to Teays Hill in 1842, adds a missing page to the history of the old burying ground. —The Coalsmouth Journal, Vol. I, No. 4, published by the St. Albans Historical Society.

But I am straying from my subject, I was speaking of William Capehart, Thenie's oldest brother. When he died he left my father her guardian, and she continued to live with us at her old home "Riverside." Steve, her youngest and favorite brother, boarded with us a while. He was always a quiet good boy, while Charley, her other brother, was a wild reckless fellow but good-hearted and everyone liked him. He was

extravagant and too generous for his own good and gave away everything. He was handsome with dark hair and dark blue eyes, very straight, a fine looking figure and always dressed handsomely. Before he was of age he traveled about from city to city and got in all kinds of scrapes.

Once he went off with a band of strolling showmen and stayed with them until they got all the money he had with him, which was considerable. They slipped off one night from the hotel where they had stopped, leaving Charley to stand for the bill and him with no money. However, it was not a lesson that lasted very long as he was taken in by the next rascal that came along.

He was a young man who was an artist pretending to be painting a panorama of the Mississippi River. He said he was too poor and could not raise the two hundred dollars he needed to finish it. Charley borrowed the money for him and he promised to repay him when he finished the picture. It was no trouble for Charley to get the money as everyone knew he would come into a large estate when he became of age. When the fellow got the money he went off to finish the painting and as I remember Charley never saw or heard tell of him afterwards.

What Mollie never knew was that a young artist named John Banvard actually did paint a panorama picture of the Mississippi River. He floated down the entire course of the river making sketches. He began his painting in an old barn in Louisville, Kentucky, and when completed it was a three-mile-long canvas. he went broke several times and had to stop to raise money in order to finish it in 1841. Probably Charley Capehart's two hundred dollars would have bought a lot of canvas at that time. The painting was exhibited in America and abroad and won world-wide acclaim. It also made John Banvard a wealthy man.

In the spring of 1852, there was a young man from Loudoun County, Virginia, who came to the neighborhood. He had just become of age and got his part of his father's estate and had come west to locate in some kind of business. He was stopping at the hotel where Charley Capehart was boarding and Charley brought him to our house to introduce him to his sister

By Forrest Hull.

and myself. His name was Andy Anderson and he visited our house regularly after that and addressed me. I imagined I loved him and engaged myself to him, but Father did not approve of it. He said we knew nothing of him only what he had told himself and he thought it best to wait.

So Andrew went to Illinois and there located in a town in the northwestern part of the state. We corresponded regularly but after he was gone for six months or more I found I did not love him as I should one I would marry. Therefore, I thought I should break my engagement, but when I first proposed it he would not hear of it at all. So he went on corresponding insisting that I not return my ring and he would not return my letters. Realizing that I was persuaded to it he decided to come on and see me. I told him not to do it and then I quit answering his letters. It was a big undertaking and very expensive at that time to come from where he was to here as there were no railroads. in defense of myself, I must say that he was the only man I ever engaged myself to except the one I married.

About this time there was a young preacher in the Northern Methodist Church sent to our place. His name was Timothy Taylor and he was from Loudoun County, Virginia, near where Mr. Anderson was from. Taylor was young and very poor and had just commenced preaching, I believe that was only his second year. He seemed to be a good devoted Christian, but Father never liked him as he had no confidence in him. When he began to pay particular attention to Thenie, Father cautioned her but we soon found out she thought more of him than any of her other beaus. When her brothers found out he was addressing her they also objected and begged her not to have anything to do with him and pointed out that he only wanted her property. All the objections only made things worse and she engaged herself to him.

It was against the rules of his church for him to own slaves and she owned several that were hired out. She was greatly attached to them as if they were her own relations and would not have sold one under any condition. Mr. Taylor was mean enough and fool enough to try to get her to sell them before they were married. This way he would have the money and would not have to free them as he knew the church would require him to do. He was afraid to bring the subject to her but was fool enough to talk to others about it. Being where one of her boys "Gus" was hired, Taylor remarked that "Miss Thenie was going to sell him," which he overheard. Gus came immediately to see his Miss Thenie, whom he almost worshipped, and told her what he had heard. It shocked her and made her so angry that she at once attacked Taylor about it. But he was a smooth-tongued hypocrite and explained it all away declaring that Gus was entirely mistaken. Of course, Thenie believed him as she loved him and informed him if they were married the slaves would be freed and not sold.

A few months later we heard Mr. Taylor was addressing another lady, a member of his church, who he thought had more property. However, she soon discharged him. All this was while he was still engaged to Thenie, but she refused to believe it. It was then in the spring of 1853 and Dr. McGinnis began to address her and she engaged herself to him although she did not care a cent for him. She did it out of revenge because she thought he had treated me badly. He had been making love to me ever since he came to this place even though we were never engaged. I had gone on a visit to Paint Creek and was from home some time. It was while I was gone he set in to making love to her and hurried and was engaged before my return. Soon after my return he called one morning and she laughed at him and told him it had all been a joke and that she had never cared for him. Oh, he was perfectly furious and she told me afterwards that she felt afraid of him. Of course I had nothing more to do with him either, except in the most distant, polite manner.

Courtship and Marriage

IT WAS IN THE SPRING of 1853 that Dr. John Walls came to Kanawha from Winchester, Virginia, on business for his Aunt Jane Watkins. She was a maiden lady that lived with his father and she owned a large tract of land out here on the Kanawha. It was what was known as the Washington farm and is now owned by Simon Staton, just below Red House. It was through her writing out here to Uncle James Teays that we first heard of the Walls family. They were relatives of the Teays' on their mother's side, she explained that our great-grandmothers were sisters.

Miss Jane Watkins wrote her first letter to my Uncle James in 1843 and after he had moved to Missouri, Uncle Joe Capehart found the letter with some of his old papers. Wanting to know more about the relationship he wrote and told her all he knew about her land and asked for her information about the family. He was so delighted when he received an answer from her niece, Miss Bettie Walls, that he came by the school house and read it to all of his nieces during recess. He then asked us all to write a few lines to put with his reply. We did so and when she wrote again she inquired about each one of us by name and asked us to write. For several years Cousin Bettie (Chilton) Wilson and myself kept up a regular correspondence. It was in 1852 she wrote that her brother, Dr. John Walls who was a widower, had read our letters and would like to correspond with one of us since he expected to come out here to see to business for his aunt. By that time Cousin Bettie was married and was living up Elk and asked me to write to Dr. Walls. This I did and we got up quite a flirtation on paper. First, he sent a Harpers Magazine which was new to me and then a box of flowers. When he finally came I felt as if I already knew him.

He came very unexpectedly the last of April while I was sick in bed with a cold. Thenie who was at the window of our upstairs room exclaimed "Oh, Mollie, here comes such a nice looking gentleman in the gate." Father was on the front veranda talking with Uncle Samuel Wilson when the gentleman came up to them and introduced himself as Dr. Walls of Winchester, Virginia. As Thenie could hear every word that was said it excited us very much. She said, "Now Moll you must get up and go down to see him since you have been writing to him." I said, "no, you must go," but just about this time Aunt Thenie Wilson came in having heard that I was sick and brought me some syrup for my cold. She had passed Dr. Walls on the veranda and was very much pleased with his appearance. She was mortified that brother John and Mr. Wilson should be entertaining him out on the porch in their everyday working clothes.

We agreed that Thenie must go down and invite him in the parlor and ask him to stay all night and not go back to the hotel. Thenie went with the understanding that I should dress and be ready to see him by supper. When she came back she was pleased and said she liked him but that he was too old for a beau. She thought he was so intelligent and refined in his manners and although he was not handsome he was fine looking and dressed so well.

After supper I went down in the parlor and met him for the first time. After corresponding for a year I had formed an opinion of him in which I was not disappointed. No one could help respecting him at first sight. He was so dignified, I knew he was one that the more you saw of him the better you would like him. I was not so young in years, as I was twenty-three, but I was young in experience. I was very childish in many things and doubted if he would fancy me for a wife. Therefore, I felt easy in his company and did my best to make his visit pleasant. The girls all teased me so about writing to him and I told them I would never marry a widower for nothing in the world. As Father often said though "We do not know what we will do until the time comes," and so it was in this case.

Dr. Walls stayed a week or more. He went to Putnam to see his aunt's land and met with several lawyers. He also visited all of his relations at Coalsmouth and everyone liked him. We took long rides and the country looked beautiful.

THERE WAS NOT MUCH of a town at that time where St. Albans is now. Mr. P. R. Thompson had laid off all the bottom land in town lots and sold some off, calling the place "Phillipi." He lived in the large old house on the hill that looked like an old English castle with its stone columns and Virginia creeper covered over the front. There was only a half-dozen or more houses then. Two brothers named Seashole had built a carriage factory and Allen Smith had built a small dwelling and a store house. There was Mr. Lasley's house and store, both very small, and Mr. Vickers' house. This, including the Episcopal church, constituted the town at that time. On the lower side of Coal River was a village equally as small. The post office was called "Coal Bridge" which included both sides of the river.

Of course, it looked small and rustic to Dr. Walls who had been in all the large eastern cities and also lived in a large town. Yet he seemed to be pleased with our country, it was the first time he had ever been in western Virginia.

During the time he was here he addressed me and proposed marriage. The wedding was set for July or August with him returning home until that time. It was such a long and tedious journey in the stage he thought it unnecessary and expensive to return more than once. But I was young and foolish and would not hear to being married on just his second visit, and required him to come three times. He came out again in July and returned then again the last week in August to be married.

Cousin Thenie and myself went to Cincinnati to get our wedding outfits as we had agreed to be married the same day. She to Timothy Taylor, the Methodist preacher, and I to Dr. Walls. We went to Cincinnati in June and my Uncle Alvah Hansford and my Cousin Sallie Hansford went with us as company and they also helped select our things. You could not buy many ready-made things at that time as you do now. We each bought our wedding dresses, silver gray silk, mine brocaded in a white leaf and Thenie's plain. Our traveling dresses were dark Irish poplin, trimmed in black velvet ribbon and lace with perfectly plain tight fitting waist and plain skirt. Then a deep cape trimmed with six rows of narrow black velvet ribbon. We each bought two thin dresses and a white wedding bonnet. We also got a traveling bonnet and a small cottage white straw. The wedding bonnet was white lace trimmed in white roses with a white veil and white satin ribbons. It was considered beautiful by everyone. We also got white kid gloves and white silk stockings.

We enjoyed our trip very much, going and coming on the steamboat which was elegantly furnished and with the best of eating. We would sit out on the guards in the evening and sing. Cousin Sallie Hansford had a sweet voice and so did Thenie.

Mrs. P. R. Thompson, Jr. went down on the boat with us also. She was going to get Sue Thompson's wedding outfit. She always wanted us to sing as she was very sad since her husband was in California looking for a home for them, and they were entirely broken up.

Mrs. Roote Thompson was the wife of Philip R. Thompson, Jr., oldest son of Col. Philip R. and Sarah (Slaughter) Thompson.

The 1850 Census of Kanawha County lists the family as follows:

Philip R. Thompson · 53 years old · farmer · born in Virginia, estate valued at $10,000.

<u>Wife</u> Sarah · 45 years old · born in Virginia.

<u>Children</u> Philip, 19 · Susan, 17 · George H., 15 · Lucy, 14

<u>At Home</u> Elisa, 9 · Lillias, 7 · Ellen, 5 · George, 3.

Philip R. Thompson, Sr. died at Coalsmouth in 1837 and the major part of his estate went to his wife, Sarah. She was listed in the Census of 1850 as living with another son, Dr. John Thompson. It was noted that the value of her estate was $97,000, a considerable amount for the time and place.

Mrs. R. Thompson did not return with us, we did not see her any more after we left the boat. She went to her brother's in Covington and we went to the hotel in Cincinnati. While we were there Uncle Alvah proposed going to see a relation of ours living in Covington. She was Mrs. Kincaid who was a Miss Manacer. He did not have their address but he persuaded us that it made no difference as Covington was so small that he had no idea there was more than one family by that name. After dinner this hot day in June, we crossed the ferry as there was no bridge then. We inquired of the ferryman if he knew a family by that name and he directed us to a nearby house. We went there and found a Mrs. Kincaid who was a perfect stranger. She directed us to another house several blocks off but they were strangers also. I wanted to go back to Cincinnati but Uncle Alva said he knew the next place would be the right one. So we walked on and went to no less than four or five different families and then had to give it up as it was late in the evening. We finally returned to the ferry and just as we were going on board we met Mr. Kincaid coming off and he insisted that we return with him. As he lived on the edge of town almost a mile from the ferry, I was so tired and worn out when I got there I did not enjoy the visit. I had on light silk gaters and the bottoms had worn clear through to my naked foot. All the shoes at that time were without heels, I suppose that was the reason. We returned to the hotel the next day and then to the boat where I got a good rest by the time I got home.

When Thenie and I returned we went to making our wedding clothes. We had no sewing machines then and it all had to be done by hand. We hired out some of it. We told no one we were fixing to be married except Father. Almost all the relations thought Thenie would marry Mr. Taylor but they did not expect me to marry Dr. Walls. He came back to see me in July and brought me several handsome presents. One was a nice breast pin or broach with his likeness in it and it cost fifteen dollars, the one my daughter Mamie has now. I would not take it then and told him to keep it until we were married as I would not take fine gifts from gentlemen. He also brought me a plain heavy gold ring for our wedding agreement ring. He again wanted to be married at that time. I look back now and see how foolish it was in me not to have married him then instead of making him spend so much time going and coming when I already knew all about him, but I was young and proud.

After Dr. Walls had left I made my annual visit to Paint Creek to see Grandmother and Bettie Hansford. I told Grandmother that I was to be married and who to and she was pleased when she found out he was a relation of my mother's. She asked me what color were his eyes and when I said blue, she said he is all right. Then she took off her wedding ring and gave it to me, she said that I was the only granddaughter she would give it to. She said she had drawn the warp of her wedding dress through it when Johnny had given it to her and she had worn it ever since.

It was worn very thin and I was afraid to wear it continually for fear of breaking it so I kept it in a box with other things that I prized. Years after I was married my sister Cint who was staying with me at the time, put it on and lost it. I grieved over the loss for a long time and always will regret it. Although if I had it now no one would value it as I did. The longer I live the more I see that it is no use to hoard up things for following generations here in America where there is continual moving and changing. In England and Europe where landed property is entailed, they can keep things together for at least a few generations.

WE STILL KEPT our marriage a secret as Dr. Walls lived so far away and was so uncertain about the time he could get here.

One day Thenie and I were sitting in the parlor with all the shutters closed to keep it cool, when Nellie, the house servant came to the door and said there is a Gypsy fortune teller out here that wants to come in and tell your fortunes. I said no, I already know all I want to know. While I was speaking, the Gypsy who was just behind Nellie, pushed into the room. "Oh, yes lady, I will tell you everything," she said. I said I had nothing to pay her but she said clothes would do, such as a dress. I told her I had no dress but she said how about that red dress hanging upstairs in your room." I then asked Nellie why she had let her upstairs. She replied she had not been upstairs and that she had never seen her before she came in the door a few minutes before.

Thenie spoke up and said she would give her a dress. But the Gypsy replied, "Oh, no, lady, bad luck to take dress from you, black mourning." Thenie was in black for her brother. She insisted on seeing my hand, said if she did not tell me something true that I need not pay her. I held out my hand, she looked and said, "you have no mother and you are going to be married this year." She looked toward Thenie and said, "you think that you and that lady will be married on the same day but you will not." We looked at each other and laughed. I then asked her to tell me the given name of the one I am to marry. Even Thenie did not know as he always signed his name J. W. Walls, but she answered "John" which was correct. Thenie said it was such a common name that she had only guessed. So she asked her to tell her the name of the one she was to marry. The Gypsy looked at her and said "Timothy." She then told her that she would have no little ones and that she would never comb a grey head. She told me I was going far away over mountains and rivers, and said I would live in a large white house with plenty of servants. She added that when the poor old Gypsy comes by they will sick the dogs on her.

Thenie said you did not tell me a good fortune and I have a notion not to pay you a cent. We paid her though and laughed over it for some time. However, a few weeks before we were to be married, Mr. Taylor found he could not marry at that time as it was the same time as Conference. Thenie then had to give up the idea and we both remembered what the Gypsy had told us.

I was married the 31st of August 1853. Dr. Walls came on several days before that he might make all necessary preparations for our journey. He went to Charleston and hired a hack and driver to take us as far as the White Sulphur in Greenbrier County.

The evening before I wrote a note to my friend, Mary Lasley, for her and Sallie to come down and stay all night with me as my cousin from Winchester, Virginia was here and I wished them to get acquainted with him. They came and we spent such a pleasant evening with Dr. Walls and Charley Capehart in the parlor. When we went upstairs to my room there set my trunk newly marked with my name, all packed and strapped. Mary looked and then threw herself on the bed and commenced crying. She said, "Oh, Mollie, I did not think you would treat me so as not to tell me you were married and going so far away. I then told her I was afraid something would happen that Dr. Walls would not get here. We soon got her to laughing and she forgave me.

I see now I did not do right by not telling my dearest friend and also my sisters. I should have told Vic at least and explained it to her and been more like a sister should be. Yet it was not altogether my fault. I had, as it were, been alone all my life until Thenie came. Also, the Negroes had taught me to hide everything and I have not gotten over it, even now. I take pleasure in doing things secretly and then showing it afterwards. It is not that I am benefiting myself in any way. I never tell others any personal matters as most women delight in doing. Mr. Rust always said it had been his way all his life. He said he never received any benefit from others advice as they usually wanted to benefit themselves. Yet I think we can carry it too far as we often wound the feelings of our friends unintentionally. They think we are trying to hide something from them when it is merely a habit.

Oh well, to go back to my marriage. I sent a servant around to ask my aunts, uncles, and cousins to come at nine o'clock in the morning. They were all there that could come and the older ladies thought it was dreadful for me to marry and go so far away. They said they knew I would not live a year as I was so delicate. When the ceremony was being performed they were all crying. Of course it made me feel dreadful, but I only gave way for a minute or so. I was laughing when I went upstairs to change my dress for traveling.

By that time the hack was at the front gate looking very stylish with its pretty white trimmings, white horses, and a black driver. I bid farewell to all, feeling very sad, but not showing it. I had such perfect confidence in Dr. Walls that I felt it would be my own fault if I was not happy. I only regretted going so far away. When I think of it now and think how merciful and kind the good Lord was to me, I feel as if I could never thank Him enough.

I bade them all farewell as cheerful as I could. All the servants crowded about me asking if I was going to take any of them with me. I told Jane that I could never think of taking her when her husband could not go. Dr. Walls had servants enough.

As we passed my friends houses, they all came out to wave goodbye. As we passed Ravenswood, Cousin Frazier Hansford's old place, the Thornton family who lived there then were all out on the brow of the hill to wave goodbye. That was the last time I ever saw Sallie Thornton who I thought so bright and pretty. Oh, what a sad life hers was and how unfortunate she was. We next bid goodbye to Mr. Robert Hudson's son Willis, who was one of my admirers. He was sitting in the yard and had not heard of my marriage. He jumped up and ran to the fence but we were going fast and I only bowed, and that was the last time I saw him.

We went on to Charleston for dinner and I only remember that we had soft peaches and cream which is all I ate. We went on to Malden that night and as it had been very warm and bright all morning, it rained in the evening. While passing one of the salt furnaces, a man came out in his shirt sleeves all coveed with soot. As he came toward the road I saw it was Uncle Norris Whittaker and I asked Dr. Walls to stop so I could bade him goodbye. He said he was glad I stopped and said there were not many girls in my place that would have done it. He said he had no idea of seeing me and would not have pushed himself on my notice if he had.

Dr. Walls said that he was a poor being that few girls would have recognized. I told him he was my Uncle Norris and that I was not ashamed of my relations. I then explained that he was my step-mother's brother-in-law who had always been so kind to me when I boarded there as a child, I would not forget it.

THE NEXT DAY was the first day of September, 1853. We went on and the next place we stopped was at Uncle Morris Hansford's. He kept the toll gate on the road opposite Paint Creek, now known as Dego. Uncle Morris came down the steps to the carriage to get the toll. When he saw me he was so surprised that he scarcely knew what to say. I introduced him to Dr. Walls and inquired for Aunt Kitty and Cousin Bettie. He said they had both gone over to Grandmother's to see Uncle Gat who they thought dying. He insisted on Dr. Walls stopping and going over as he could do him some good. Dr. Walls told him that if he had been sick as long as he said and was so low, it would be of no use and that he could do him no good. So we bid Uncle Morris goodbye and I never saw him but once afterward.

Tyree Tavern built at Ansted in 1810, was headquarters of Union troops 1861–62. Dr. and Mollie Walls stayed here on their wedding tour in 1857. It was still satnding in 1996. PHC

We went on to Gauley Bridge that night. We stopped to dine at a place where they were drying peaches. They were so nice, peeled and dried in the sun. Dr. Walls bought a half bushel. I remember he gave her a little gold dollar and it was the first she had ever seen. The place we stayed in Gauley Bridge was not at all nice so we started very early and went three miles to breakfast. It was an old house but everything was so nice and sweet and we had a delightful breakfast. We only saw two old people, I left my fan there.

That night we stayed at Tyree's high up in the mountains. I remember very little about that place as we left very early in the morning.

Tyree's Tavern was known as "Halfway House" and it is still standing on the east side of Ansted. It was a regular stage stop on the James River and Kanawha Turnpike.

The original dwelling was built on the site before the Revolution and it was enlarged by William Tyree in 1810. During the winter of 1861-62, it was the headquarters for the Chicago Gray Dragoons. —West Virginia Highway Markers; W. Va. Historic Commission, 1967.

As neither Dr. or myself knew anything about the road, we depended on the old black driver to tell us and to stop wherever he thought best. We soon found out he was looking out more for the horses getting good feed than for us. That day we stopped at a house of entertainment at the forks of the road where it turns off to go to Blue Sulphur. Everything looked dirty and sloven, the table was in the room with a bed. It was a hot summer day and they had fried ham and eggs and had hot biscuits with some preserves. There seemed to be a house full of women, I did not see a man but Dr. saw one in the yard. One of the women heard me call him Doctor and she left the room and we could hear her telling the other women that they must come in and see. One of them seemed to be complaining with stomach trouble for which she asked his advice and if he had any medicine that would do her any good. She said she was teaching school and was not able to do anything else. Said the nearest doctor was ten miles and he was at the springs and would not practice in the country. Dr. Walls told her she ought to diet herself and she should live on milk or weak tea and crackers and take more exercise. Every time he would tell her something she would turn to the other women and say "I told you so."

Blue Sulphur Springs in 1859. Just prior to the war this famous health resort was turned into a Baptist College. During the war, the spa was used by both armies as a hospital. In the winter of 1862–63, several hundred Georgia troops were encamped here. Eighty-nine of them died of a typhoid fever epidemic and were buried on top of the hill in coffins made out of benches from the cottages and buildings of the resort. In 1864 Union troops burned down the rest of the buildings. PHC

We went from there to Blue Sulphur which was a pretty place and a great many people from Kanawha were there. At that time it was the favorite resort of the Charleston folks as scarcely any of them went to the White.

From there we went to Lewisburg and put up at Stalnaker's Hotel to stay over Sunday, as Doctor would not travel on Sunday. That was a nice place and we went to church. I left my room locked but when we returned I found that someone had been in it. I had a fine gold locket that looked like a watch, with a silk guard to it containing a gold pencil. There was also a large set ring that I did not want to wear and a gold toothpick that had been a present and I thought so much of it. It was all gone, had been taken off and I never got anything back. I acted very childish and foolish here and Dr. Walls got out of patience with me I know, although he said very little.

Monday morning we went on to White Sulphur, that was ten miles from there. Mr. I. Truslow, the man who we hired the hack from, had followed us up with a fine buggy and two beautiful dark gray horses, they were twin colts. He tried to get Dr. Walls to buy them to take us on home as we had agreed to give up the hack at Lewisburg or White Sulphur. We expected we would find many stages coming and going but we found them all full.

At the White we put up at Frazier's Hotel on the hill above the spring. Here we stayed several days trying to get on a stage. We went down to the ballroom at night. Miss Sarah Frazier found out I was a Hansford and she came to my room to see me. She asked me to go with her to watch some of the fashionable bells dance. There was a great crowd that year from all of the large cities. Bonaparte, his wife and child, were there from Baltimore. I tell you they put on style, he looked very much like his uncle, Napoleon B. His wife was fine looking when she went out horseback riding with him. She had on a black velvet riding habit that buttoned up in front with diamonds.

The child rode in an open carriage with its nurse and a Negro driver.

The Bonaparte that Mollie Walls saw at White Sulphur Springs was Jerome, the son of Napoleon's brother Jerome, and Elizabeth Patterson.

In 1803, while in service with the French Navy, Jerome Bonaparte visited the United States and married Elizabeth Patterson of Baltimore, without the consent of his family. After living in Baltimore for two years, Capt. Bonaparte and his wife sailed for Europe in 1805. On reaching Lisbon, a French frigate was there to prevent her landing. Jerome left his wife and went to Paris to plead her cause with the Emperor, while the ship proceeded to Amsterdam. At the entrance to the harbor two man-of-war ships awaited her and Elizabeth Bonaparte was forced to go back and seek asylum in England.

A few days after arrival in England, her son Jerome Napoleon Bonaparte was born. Here she remained awaiting the resolution of her marriage. Napoleon applied to Pope Pius VII to dissolve the marriage but the Pontiff steadfastly refused. A decree of divorce was then passed by the Imperial French Council of State. A lifetime pension of 60,000 francs a year was granted to Elizabeth and her son and they returned to Baltimore.

The father married Princess Catherine of Wurtemberg in 1807 and he then became King of Westphalia. The son graduated at Harvard in 1826 and married a Miss Williams of Roxbury, Massachusetts. Through his inheritances, Jerome Bonaparte became one of the richest men in Baltimore, where he died in 1870. —Appletons' Cyclopaedia of American Biography.

When Miss Frazier and myself went to the ballroom, she dressed in white with a great deal of trimmings. She wore a gold chain, earrings, bracelets, and her fingers were crowded with rings. Her hair was curled with flowers and I thought her over dressed. I determined to look as plain as possible. I wore a dotted Swiss, made infant waist, a white sash, a few white flowers at my waist with a white faination on my head. My hair was crimped in front and combed back plain as they wear it now. When I came out she looked at me in astonishment and said, "Are you ready?" She thought I would dress in my wedding finery I suppose. I wore no jewelry but my rings.

After we were all in the ballroom a short time, Bettie Burns came up to me. I had not seen her since she was married. She was the same light-hearted merry Bettie and seemed so glad to see me. She introduced me to her sister, Mrs. Caldwell, whose husband was part owner of the White and she insisted on me stopping sometime and making her a visit. Miss Frazier that was with me was a cousin of Bettie's and she afterwards married Mr. Summerson, a stage agent of Staunton, Virginia.

Mrs. Caldwell was the wife of William Caldwell who at that time was part owner of the resort. He had inherited his interest from his father, James Caldwell who has been referred to as the "Father of White Sulphur Springs."

James Caldwell was a sea merchant who came from Baltimore to the White Sulphur area in 1795. He married a daughter of Michael Boyer who owned the land that included the Springs. In 1816, James Caldwell became sole proprietor of the property and began the development of the White Sulphur Springs. —The White Sulphur Springs by William A. MacCorkle.

Mr. Truslow was still trying to get Dr. Walls to buy the horses and buggy which he asked five hundred dollars for. Of course, Doctor had not that much money with him. He said if I was willing to do my part by giving Truslow a check on the Kanawha Bank where I had my money, he would pay the rest. We could then proceed on our journey as there seemed no prospect of leaving then. The hotels were so crowded that the evening before we left some of the passengers on the stage stopping, slept in the stage that night with the promise of a room the next day.

We bought the horses and buggy and when we started the next morning it took two men to hold the horses while we got in. Everybody was out to see us off, the horses looked so beautiful that I never thought of danger and there really was none. After we started and drove several miles they commenced to quiet down. We had no trouble with them except they were hitched up wrong. They had been trained one for the right and one for the left and would not work any other way.

White Sulphur Springs. AC

After leaving the White we traveled slowly, stopping at noon to feed our horses and eat our lunch which we always bought where we stayed all night. The weather was delightful and I never enjoyed anything as much as our luncheon at a cool spring in the mountains. We were passing over the Alleghenies and the scenery was lovely.

We took breakfast at the Hot Springs, the hotel was on the side of the mountain. The bath houses below were near the spring and there were very few there except invalids. We next stopped at the Warm Springs and also the Bath Alum, that was a beautiful place.

After we passed Staunton we were on the macadamized pike leading up the Shenandoah Valley. It was at that time the best road I ever saw, smooth and as solid as a floor. I tell you with our two fast horses and light buggy, we traveled fast. We had put all our baggage on the stage except one small trunk, my band box, and Doctor's box.

It was now about the 15th of September and we had such beautiful weather, no rain until we passed Staunton. It then rained all day and turned cold. Near Harrisonburg I had to stop and buy myself a shawl as mine was in my trunk on the stage. Doctor bought it and it was a heavy grey one large enough to cover us both. The buggy was as tight and good as any buggy could be but it continued to rain and we both got wet.

We stopped early at a house of entertainment called the "Flowering Spring." It was an old place kept by two old people named Lincoln. We found that they were relations of the Ruffners of Charleston. Everything was plain and neat and the sweetest, cleanest beds. I could hardly make the old lady believe I was Dr. Walls wife, she thought I was his daughter at first. She was so kind and made up a wood fire in my room to dry my things. She had the nicest supper, fried chicken, batter cakes, the nicest honey and all kinds of things, but those three things I remember. I was hungry and ate more than usual.

From Mollie's description, they stayed all night at one of the oldest taverns in the Shenandoah Valley. It was at Lacey Spring; formerly known as Big Spring. The structure was a two-story log house that had been a landmark since Colonial times.

Bath Alum Springs hotels and cottages. PHC

In 1833 David Lincoln became proprieter of the old inn and in the same year his cousin, Abraham Lincoln, opened a tavern in Sagamon County, Illinois. The old tavern continued operation until 1848 when it was destroyed by fire. —Twenty-Five Chapters on the Shenandoah Valley by John Wayland

At that time I was a very small eater. I know now it was a habit, as it was not considered lady-like or nice to eat much. When I was young I never ate over one biscuit and everything else in proportion. I was always well and I never had anything the matter with my stomach in my life until almost seventy. I think people have bad habits of overloading their stomachs and that is why there is so much complaining now of stomach trouble.

The place we stopped was just this side of New Market. The country along there was beautiful, such large farms, with stone fences on each side of the Pike all the way. The next morning when we left it was bright and we drove fast as we wanted to get to Mount Jackson early. We expected to stay all night with a friend of Doctor's living there named Doctor Jourdan. Long before we got there it began to rain again and we drove very fast. When we arrived at the house I ran in dripping wet. Doctor went to get my trunk, and lo! we had lost it off of the back of the buggy. Dr. Jourdan proposed to send back and look on the road as there were few houses, but Doctor said he would rather go himself. He got on one of the horses and started but met a colored man coming with it. He was out in the field at work and saw the trunk fall off. He went immediately and asked permission to get it and follow us with it on a horse. We were so glad to get it that Dr. Walls paid him well. It was so honest in him to bring it, most darkies would not have done it.

Dr. Jourdan's folks were very kind and pleasant, one of his daughters visited us afterwards. We expected to get home that day, but did not arrive until about sundown. Doctor's house was the last house in town, at the northeast end. Therefore, we drove all the way through town, which was a mile. Everybody knew Dr. Walls but they did not expect to see him come home with a wife in a buggy. As we drove by they would run out and look after us. As the stage had already passed and we were not in it, his home folks had given up on us.

His sister Bettie was there to receive me. Mary, the colored cook, had told them what to expect by turning the coffee cup with grounds. She was full of fun and said she told Miss Bettie we would come in a private conveyance and would be there that evening. They almost carried me in the house and soon had a nice supper. All the servants seemed so well trained and so respectful and everything was so nice. Dr. Wall's sister Bettie was very affectionate and kind. I was so tired that night I soon retired. Mine was a large room with three large windows, two looking east and one looking south. That made it cheerful and healthy. The room was beautifully furnished, had a large curtain bedstead with lemon colored curtains, with pink roses and a green vine running over. There was another smaller bed, more fashionable, made all in white. There was a beautiful white china chamber set, a nice dressing case and an ingrain carpet. The curtains were white muslin and there were two vases and a lamp on the mantle. Lamps were not generally used at that time. The oil we use now was not known then.

The next morning the Doctor's sister showed me all over the house. It was a large square frame house filled in with brick, making it very substantial. It had an ell with a long porch running the full length of the house. There was a wide hall running between the main building and the ell with Venetian shutters at the end instead of doors. They opened into a flower garden where there were some rare trees and shrubbery. Among the rest was a fig tree about ten feet high. The ell contained the kitchen and the cook's room. The window of her room looked out into the garden and was completely covered with running roses. There was a high board fence between the garden and kitchen yard that was almost hid by the trees and vines. In the center of the garden were beds of annuals of all kinds, everything was beautiful.

Cousin Bettie (that is what I called Doctor's sister as she was a third or fourth cousin) was older than her brother. She was full of life and a great talker, and would ask me every few minutes how I liked my new home. The dining room was just to my notion, it had two large windows looking east. I always liked the sunlight in a dining room in the morning, it is so cheerful It was a bright room with a fire place in one corner, a door opening into the hall and one into the Doctor's office. There was a round table in the middle of the floor with a white drugget, with bunches of roses over it. Under the table was always kept a "crumb cloth" of white linen.

There was a large beautiful sideboard of mahogany that cost sixty dollars. On this was a quantity of fine glass and silver and also two large pewter pitchers that were very old and had been in the family for a long while. Everything on the sideboard was kept shiny by a Negri *(Negri'to—A member of any number of dwarfish Negroid peoples, found in Central and Southern Africa.)* man of seventy-nine, but was a boy in his size. It was his work to keep everything pertaining to that room in perfect order.

The hall was wide and was covered with black and white oil cloth. There was a pretty stairway covered with a fine carpet with wide brass rods. At the head of the stairs was a small room used as a store room and the stairsteps going to the attic were in this room. Also on two sides there were shelves, from the floor to the ceiling stowed full of all kinds of fruits, preserved and dried. We had no canned fruit then. There were also pickles of all kinds and several jars of beautiful honey. Dr. Walls had everything prepared for the winter knowing I would get there too late to see to it. There were several large four-gallon jars packed full of dried cherries, packed in sugar. I had never seen any before and I liked them better than raisins. I used to keep my pocket full all the time, oh! they were nice.

There were two bed rooms upstairs besides mine, one was William's and one the guest cham-

The Valley Pike. JWSV

    Recollections *and* Reflections *of* Mollie Hansford

ber. The parlor was a very large handsome room with an open wood fireplace that had high brass andirons and a brass fender. There was a pretty mantle piece with beautiful lamps with long glass pendants and also two tall china vases. There was a large window on each side of the fireplace, looking out on the flower garden. They had blue curtains trimmed with blue and gold fringe. The furniture and carpet were almost new, just as it was before his wife's death.

As William was in Winchester going to school, there was no one in the house but Doctor and the servants and they only used part of the house. Doctor had two children, William who was fifteen years old and was his first wife's child, and Mary Octavia, (we always called her Mollie) who was three years old. Her mother was his second wife and died at her birth. She was a sweet child and had very pretty dark brown hair. Doctor had a colored woman hired to nurse and tend to her altogether. She did nothing else except attend to my room. She was free and a bright mulatto. She was as refined and nice in manners as most of the white ladies. Her name was Cornelia Fletcher and Mollie was fond of her. I had but one objection to her and that was she did not want me to have any control of Mollie in any way, not even to say what she should wear.

Mollie's step-son, William Walls, was born in Harpers Ferry in 1837. He attended Winchester Academy and later enrolled at Winchester Medical College. He studied under Dr. Hugh M. McGuire and graduated when only 19. He remained at the college as a professor until the Civil War broke out.

Enlisting as a surgeon in the Confederate Army, he was assigned to Stonewall Jackson's Brigade. When General Jackson was wounded, he assisted Dr. McGuire in the operation when his arm was removed. Dr. Coleman administered the anesthetic, Dr. McGuire did the cutting, and Dr. Walls tied the arteries.

After the war, Dr. William Walls entered into general practice with Dr. Joseph E. Clagett in Baltimore. He also became a professor at Washington Medical College.

In 1886, while he was on a trip to Philadelphia, Dr. Walls suffered a heart attack. He died the next day at the early age of 49, having never married.

MOLLIE HAD A GREAT MANY nice clothes, her mother had been very fashionable and fond of dress. She had lived most of her life in and near Washington, D. C. She was a widow and had two sons when Dr. Walls married her. The boys were living with their father's relations. Their father was Dr. Wooten and her children went back to her old home in D. C. She was later on a visit to her cousin's in Winchester where Dr. Walls met her. She was a beautiful and highly educated woman but had a very unhappy disposition. She only lived five or six years.

William's mother was a Miss Littler, her father was a farmer and lived near Capon Springs. Dr. Walls met her when he first started out to practice medicine. She was of an admirable sweet disposition, but was delicate and died with consumption. She only lived six or seven years. She had three children and the two youngest died with scarlet fever.

Dr. Walls first located at Harpers Ferry, the U. S. Army was there at that time and there were hundreds of workmen. He had a splendid practice and only left there on the account of his wife's health. From there he moved to Newtown or Stephensburg, seven miles south of Winchester, where he continued to live until his death. He did not believe in moving about and his father lived in Winchester and never had moved. When I married Dr. Walls, his father and mother were both dead. His two maiden sisters continued to live at their old home place where they were born and raised.

Their maiden aunt, Jane Watkins, lived with them. She was upwards of seventy when I went there. She was very refined and intelligent and had traveled about a great deal and she knew all the great men. I loved to hear her talk and tell of old times. She had kept the history of the family and had traced the relationship to our family. She had been engaged to a Dr. William Teays, a nephew of our grandfather but he died very young and she never married. I can see now as she looked when I first saw her. She looked young and had been very pretty. She was small with very delicate features. She wore a turbin of white mull, pulled through a large gold ring on one side. This ring had been her grandfather Teays'. It was brought form France and had a motto in it. It was what Ruth said unto Nan:

"Where thy goeth I will go." She was dressed in a plain neat fitting black silk with a soft white muill handkerchief around her neck and crossed on her breast. She lived five or six years after my marriage.

The old homestead in Winchester had been left to Bettie and Maria by their father. It was a sweet old place on the corner of Braddock Street with an acre of ground and old-fashioned garden full of fruit and flowers, surrounded by large old trees. They certainly lived a quiet peaceful life. They never did anything but tend to their household affairs, sew a little, visit and attend church. They were devoted Christians, Bettie and Maria were Methodists while Aunt Jane was Episcopalian. Dr. Walls went back and forth every week to attend to their wants.

William boarded with them and attended the Academy. He was their pet and idol. He generally came out home once a week. He would walk out every Friday evening and back on Sunday evening. He had a beautiful dog named Rover that he thought a great deal of and he was very fond of hunting. He would generally spend his time in hunting or teaching Rover all kinds of tricks. When Rover was but a pup he taught him to fetch and carry. If he dropped anything Rover was trained to get it and bring it to him. He could give him a basket and send him to the post office which was a half mile from us and he would always bring the mail back safe. He was a black and white New Foundland, very large. He would always run by our carriage and as soon as we would get out he would jump in and let no one touch anything. He was one the best dogs I ever saw.

Once I went to Winchester to purchase things for a fair and festival that the ladies were going to have for the church. I had the money in my pocketbook which I put in a small basket. In some way I lost the basket out of the carriage and never missed it. I also noticed Rover was not running by the carriage. I asked Henry what had happened to him and he stopped the carriage and looked back. Henry said he could just see Rover coming over the hill and he seemed to have something in his mouth. When he came near enough we could see it was my basket. Then I was scared knowing all my money as well as

Locust Grove-Rock Branch was Mollie's home where she died. AC

fifty dollars of the church's money was in it. Henry commenced to call him and hold out his hand but he would not go to him but ran around to my side and leaped up and gave it to me. He seemed to know as well as I did that it was mine. Poor old fellow, how we all loved him, William had his photo taken and we still have it now. When William left to go in the army in sixty-one it was as hard to part with Rover as any of us.

One day during the war, Rover was lying on the pavement in front of our door when a Yankee soldier came by and stuck his bayonet through his shoulder. It was just in wanton cruelty as the dog was not even noticing him. We did all we could for his wound but it would not cure up as he was old. He lingered for months and would want to stay in the house with the family all the time although he had a nice house of his own. One morning we found him lying on the doorstep dead. As Henry, our colored boy said, who had taught him as much as his master; "we buried him in the garden with honors."

Whatever reasons Mollie may have had for writing her "Recollections," a publication such as this was probably not one of them. It is reflected in her casual straightforward style that her writings were probably only a simple pleasure she had found in reliving the past during her old age.

Epilogue

After Mollie married Dr. Walls in 1853, she went to Newtown near Winchester, Virginia, to live. She was there all during the Civil War and at least ten crucial battles were fought within a few miles of her home. Since she lived on the Valley Pike she literally saw much of the war go by her front door. She later wrote an account of her life during the war which has been published under separate cover.

After the death of her husband, Dr. Walls, Mollie returned to the Kanawha Valley with her two young children, Hansford and Mamie. In 1878 she married Major Vincent Redman Rust, a widower who lived in Putnam County. The Rust estate was called "Locust Grove" and was located at Rock Branch. The home later became the Club House of the Rock Branch Golf Course. It was here that she began writing her "Recollections" as a simple pleasure she had found in reliving the past to overcome the loneliness of old age.

On January 1, 1899, she wrote: "It is a dark, gloomy day as I sit alone in my room, I look back over my life and realize how many New Year's Days I have enjoyed that are now passed and gone forever. I can but think of my neglected opportunities, my misused privileges and the mistakes of my eventful life. These things cannot be recalled but are now only vain regrets.

"I thank my Heavenly Father for His many blessings as I bid the old year adieu. I welcome the New Year with many prayers that I may make better use of my remaining days, and try to do more for His glory and the good of those around me, or at least set for them a better example.

"It has been impressed on my mind for some time that I should write down the many incidents of my life for my children and grandchildren. In years to come it may be a pleasure and possibly a benefit to them in some way."

Mollie continued to write her "Recollections" as long as she was able. She died August 11, 1900, probably leaving unrecorded many other stirring incidents of her long and eventful life. She was laid to rest on the hill overlooking "Locust Grove," having been assured of her personal salvation, according to her own testimony.

Selected Bibliography

Atkinson, George W., *History of Kanawha Co.* Charleston, W. Va. *West Virginia Journal,* 1876.

Cohen, Stan. *Historic Springs of the Virginias.* Charleston, W. Va., Pictorial Hist. Pub. Co., 1987.

Comstock, Jim. *Hardesty's W. Va. Counties Kanawha and Putnam.*West Virginia Hillbilly, Richwood, W. Va., 1973.

Dayton, Ruth Woods. *Pioneers and Their Homes on the Upper Kanawha* West Virginia Pub. Co., Charleston, W. Va., 1947.

DeGruyter, Julius. *The Kanawha Spectator, Vol. I.* Jarrett Printing Co., Charleston, W. Va., 1953.

Hale, John P., *History of the Kanawha Valley,* 2 Vols. Brant, Fuller and Co., Madison, Wis., 1891.

Laidley, William S., *History of Charleston and Kanawha Co.,* Richmond Arnold Pub. Co., Chicago, 1911.

McCorkle, William A. *The White Sulpher Springs.* Neale Pub. Co., 1916.

Rice, Otis K. *Charleston and The Kanawha Valley,* Windsor Pub. Inc., Woodland Hills, CA, 1981.

St. Albans Historical Society Journal. Selected Articles, 1972–1988.

St. Albans History, Walsworth Publishing Co., 1993.

Upper Vandalia Historical Society Journal. Selected Articles, 1962–1988.

Wallace, George S., *Cabell County Annals and Families.* Garrett and Massie Pub., Richmond, 1935.

Wayland, John W. *Twenty-Five Chapters on the Shenandoah Valley.* C. J. Carrier, Harrisonburg, VA, 1976.

West Virginia Historical and Antiquarian Society Journal. Jan. 1897.

West Virginia Historical Magazine, 1901–1905. Selected Articles.

Wilson, James G. and John Fish. Six Vols. *Appleton's Cyclopedia of American Biographies.* D. Appleton Co., New York, 1888.

References as Indicated for Various Items.

Index